What people are saying about Get Organised

Carol Posener and her company Get Organised made an enormous difference to my life and even helped me recoup a lot of money … I am so busy at work, I find it very hard to keep up with all my personal paperwork and things had got out of control. I had reached a point where I could hardly bear to go into my home office and essential services were on the point of being cut off through unpaid bills lying under heaps of other junk. As well as giving me lots of practical advice and setting up systems for me that I can't actually stand to do, Carol got on with doing a lot of the things that I was so behind on. This has led me to recouping several hundred dollars in invoices, expenses and Medicare bills that I had left unclaimed. This has more than paid for Carol's services — plus I now have an office I look forward to going into. I heartily recommend Get Organised to any busy person.

Maggie Alderson — Best-selling author of Pants on Fire
and fashion columnist for Good Weekend

It is the best investment in peace of mind for the smallest amount of money I have ever made. Once it's organised it's done, and I don't have to do it ever again.

Anna Ritchie

I was daunted by the prospect of tackling all the paper, memorabilia etc. Carol's relaxed manner and sensitivity to her client's idiosyncrasies enabled me to decide freely what was really important to keep and how to keep it in a way that was both accessible and attractive.

Glynn O'Neill — Mediator/social worker

Very good — calm, efficient and helpful service.

Hilary Linstead — Film producer/theatrical agent

Get Organised!

Get Organised!

A PRACTICAL GUIDE TO ORGANISING YOUR HOME AND OFFICE

CAROL POSENER

Lothian BOOKS

Thomas C. Lothian Pty Ltd
132-136 Albert Road, South Melbourne, 3205
www.lothian.com.au

National Library of Australia
Cataloguing-in-Publication data:

Posener, Carol.
   Get organised!

   ISBN 0 7344 0331 3.

   1. Organization. 2. Storage in the home. 3. Paperwork
   (Office practice) - Management. 4. Conduct of life. I.Title.

158.1

Cover and text design by The Modern Art Production Group
Cover and text illustrations by Suzanne Maher
Typeset by The Modern Art Production Group
Printed in Australia by Griffin Press

Disclaimer
The author has made every effort to ensure that the information
contained in this book is complete and accurate. However, the
information and advice contained in this book are not intended as
a substitute for consulting a professional specialist in regards to
any action that may affect your wellbeing or property. Individual
readers must accept responsibility for their own actions, safety
and health. Neither the author nor the publisher will be liable or
responsible for any loss, injury or damage allegedly arising from
any information or suggestion in this book.

Contents

Part 1 A philosophy

Part 2 Organising your home

Part 3   Organising your office

About the author

Carol Posener established her business, Get Organised, eight years ago. Although she started her career in banking and stockbroking, she broke away from these industries in search of a business of her own, in search of her passion. On her road to self-fulfilment, she identified the need for better organisation in offices. Too much clutter and a lack of systems were the main problems.

Carol found that she enjoyed organising and designing time-saving systems. Clearing out clutter was also a major part of the process when she applied her ideas to the home. Carol believes that clearing spaces clears the mind, so people are able to move forward with their lives in a more productive way. That's how Get Organised came about.

Carol found a big demand for effective systems in the small business, SOHO (small office/home office) area and larger corporations. Many people start businesses because they have skills in a particular area, or are an 'ideas' person, but they forget to give attention to the administrative side of the business. So right from the start they don't have the systems they will need as the business develops. This comes at a cost down the track when they have trouble locating information and their office space is filling up with paperwork, all because they didn't recognise the need for systems.

Acknowledgements

To all my wonderful clients who constantly inspired me to contact that creative place in myself that allows me to access better solutions and think laterally. My work has been a pleasure because of you. You are the people who have helped my business to grow and prosper, and without you this book would never have been a consideration — so thank you.

To my gorgeous husband Mark, for his never-ending support, his constant supply of encouraging words, and the endless energy he directed to cooking dinners and organising the house the way we like it. Without his support I would not have had the time to write this book.

To my twin sister Suzanne, an extraordinary artist, whose natural, self-trained ability has inspired many and given me great joy throughout my life. How fortunate I am to have you in my life and to have you illustrate this book for me.

To Averill Chase from Lothian, who guided me throughout the nine months that I worked on this book. Thank you for your patience, intuitive knowledge about organising, and encouraging and motivating support. You certainly made my job easier.

To all the companies who provided photographs for this book, a big thankyou for the professional shots and your enthusiasm for the project.

Preface

Human beings are inquisitive and, in many civilisations, acquisitive. We strive for knowledge and for continual improvements in the resources and products that provide us with our material standard of living. New ideas are being developed every day to satisfy such desires, and there are always new goods on the market. Advertising informs us of new products and encourages us to purchase them. We may buy simply because we want the latest and greatest product, and if we can afford to do so this does not create a problem — as long as we dispose of goods we no longer need. Many of us have trouble offloading these things, and it is this accumulation that creates a problem for us — an overabundance of CLUTTER.

There are many reasons we hang onto things. The possessions that surround us may keep us happy and fulfilled; they may make us feel secure and successful. We very often keep something for fear of hurting another person's feelings — throwing it away would make us feel guilty. We may feel that if we discard something sentimental, the memories will go too. Parting with an old tapestry handbag that belonged to our mother becomes impossible because of its sentimental value, so the item is neither used nor discarded. We store items in our cupboards, attics, garages, wardrobes and drawers; we hang onto objects that we don't use or even like.

Because of our reluctance to discard possessions, many of us become hoarders. We don't even know what belongings we have in certain areas of our homes. Sifting through boxes or a shed can seem overwhelming: it's too big a job and too time-consuming. We haven't looked there for years and we've got better things to do, so we put it off.

Because many of us have become time-poor, organising ourselves and keeping on top of everything in our lives has become an enormous challenge. But the disorganisation that will most likely result causes stress — more stress than we need in our already over-stressed lives. Author Hugh Mackay writes in an article entitled, 'Whoa! Hold the stresses and live a little' (*Sydney Morning Herald*, 13 May 2000):

> It's possible to tranquillise or even anaesthetise your system so you mask the effects of stress. But it will continue to sap your energy as long as you postpone treatment of the cause. Nothing can cripple you like the feeling that you're not in control of your situation; that you are powerless; that your destiny is in someone else's hands.

We need to take back control, to do something about our stress and disorganisation, or our lives will continue to suffer. Hugh Mackay says:

This can be can be achieved, but always at a cost and only if you're determined to make the change. If you want to live in a new way, you'll have to give up some old habits and that might cause short-term pain — to yourself and others. Many men, for instance have tricked themselves into working too hard for the sake of their family's happiness and security, only to find the family would have been happier with more of their time and less of their money.

Hugh Mackay's sentiments about stress can be applied to the stress we cause in our lives by surrounding ourselves with clutter. There comes a point when we may realise that we have become blind to the things around us that clutter our lives, and that we may have a lot of work to do to get our lives back into order.

Through the accumulation of experience gained from working in my business, Get Organised, I saw a need for this book, both to provide a back-up for my existing clients and to support those who want to organise themselves better. In this book I aim to demystify organisation skills and show how easy it can be to get organised. We are all quite similar in the way we think and learn, so anyone can become organised with a little knowhow and practice.

The book is designed to add a little lightness to the weight of organising yourself. It will help you to take the first step to being an organised person. It will show you that organising yourself and your surroundings doesn't have to be a burden. In fact, it can become a joy and can give you wonderful feelings of self-satisfaction, energy, confidence and, ultimately, fulfilment. Everything you need to have in your life will be at your fingertips because you can now de-clutter your spaces and reclaim your life!

What is 'Get Organised'?

Get Organised is a service designed with the ultimate aim of saving you time in your business or home. There are many tasks that we can assist people with, including:

- moving
- restyling a room
- organising your kitchen cupboards
- reorganising your children's rooms
- reorganising the garage
- setting up a new office (home or corporate)
- establishing a new filing system or overhauling an existing system
- storing your important possessions or paperwork efficiently
- sorting out an area of your life.

What services are provided?

Get Organised has offered solutions to a range of businesses within the media, the entertainment industry, government departments, professional firms, tertiary institutions, the hospitality industry, the information technology industry and public relations firms.

Corporate or small business services

Get Organised offers a range of services to businesses:

- establishing filing systems (drawer or lateral systems)
- establishing archiving systems, including culling excess or outdated information, updating old archives and establishing new ones
- organising to improve efficiency
- creating order in storage rooms and cabinets to create space and efficiency in locating or archiving records, stationery and equipment
- creating a better presentation in your office environment
- making information accessible, creating compact lists
- updating regularly used information such as product catalogues and price lists
- developing formal office procedures so that management can assess staff performance, facilitate job sharing and cover staff leave
- establishing quality records management systems
- preparing assessment reports of your business and office to advise on areas where improvements can be made in efficiency and space utilisation
- managing office relocations, including sourcing lease or rental options, obtaining quotes from removalists, planning the move, packing up the office and setting up at the new location.

Domestic services

Many clients want assistance with organising their homes or domestic routines. Our services include:

- reorganising kitchens, cupboards and garages
- arranging garage sales
- setting up homes
- organising personal paperwork
- organising day-to-day tasks such as banking, paying bills, shopping, claiming medical expenses, setting up Internet banking and automatic payments
- writing business plans for home-based businesses
- setting up home offices
- organising stationery.

Storage is a big problem for many people so we organise cupboards, bookshelves, filing cabinets, storage rooms, garages and lofts. We provide storage advice and ideas on products to enhance productivity.

How to use this book

The main function of this book is to provide a life-long reference source for solutions to organising specific areas of your business, home or life. The book is designed so that you can either methodically work through the chapters or dip into the relevant section. For guidance refer to the table of contents or the comprehensive index at the end of the book. Special features include the step-by-step checklists, tips and case studies. There are tips on many topics, including time management, kitchens and pantries, bedrooms, children's spaces, living rooms, handy tools and equipment. There are steps to follow to set up systems such as office filing and archiving. By working down the table of contents you can tidy up and organise your whole life. Choose an area that is a priority for you and begin. This one small step is the first you will take to free yourself of clutter and chaos.

Part One
A philosophy

1 Why people need organising

> *If you do what you've always done, you'll get what you've always gotten.*
>
> Anon

We all need patterns and routines or rituals — it is human nature. If we look around us we can see patterns in everything we do and everything around us. For example, consider the human life cycle: conception, birth, life and, inevitably, death. Every living creature follows a similar pattern. In fact, this is the way all life functions — patterns repeating patterns.

Patterns and routines are the natural rhythm of everyday life. We start and finish tasks or activities so that something else can come from them, or simply to maintain this rhythm. For everything that is begun, there must be a finish. Finishing or completing a task or activity lends order to our lives — it keeps the flow of our lives moving forward. Putting things in place, like routines or little reminders, can give structure to our lives. It's just a matter of setting out to do something and seeing it through to the end. Some of us have difficulty developing that natural rhythm and need a little help along the way.

Those of us who need organising fall into a number of categories.

We may be:
- chronic clutterers
- procrastinators
- people who are afraid of change
- busy people who give a low priority to being organised
- people who are full of good intentions but never complete the task.

Organisationally-challenged people

I've often considered why my clients need my services. For many people the reasons are quite simple: they have let things get way out of hand because they lead busy lives. Some don't know how to organise themselves or their belongings and have no inclination to do so.

A few clients use my service because they are unable to deal with their lives effectively as a result of a trauma. The cause of such trauma may be an emotional blockage, a tragedy, an accident or just the difficult life they've been dealt. These people

have been unable to face their personal paperwork since that trauma, so their personal belongings are in chaos, causing them more confusion and stress. Sorting through their possessions and looking back at what happened when the trauma occurred can be a daunting and emotional process for them.

Some people use my service because their physical or mental disabilities prevent them from organising themselves effectively. Their disability may slow down their processing of everyday transactions. Those who have suffered brain injury may not be able to plan or to organise themselves. These people cannot rely on their memories to get themselves organised, so they need to have systems established that enable them to follow a routine. Once these systems are established and they have de-cluttered their personal spaces, they can continue with their lives with much more ease. They can see where everything is and know what they own and where it lives, so they are no longer hindered by disorder.

Often the elderly need help in de-cluttering their homes and establishing simple systems and processes. It can take a lot of time to put things into practice and action, as very often the aged take a lot longer than younger people to do things. This type of service helps them to organise things in their life and makes their life easier.

Why do we allow ourselves to become disorganised?

Many of us have busy lives. We are constantly bombarded with things to do — work to go to each day, skills to learn, people to see, meals to cook and eat, sport and games to play, friends to visit, relatives to catch up with, bills to pay, money to invest, movie and theatre tickets to purchase, holidays to go on, television to watch, newspapers and magazines to read, responsibilities to children, parties to plan, parties to go to, careers to start, careers to change, choices to make, and so on. So many choices!

It can all be a bit much sometimes. We only have 24 hours in the day, so how can we fit it all in? Something has to give! Our priorities have been changing ever so gradually, year after year, until all of a sudden we're in a mess. The mail now includes notices threatening disconnection of the phone line, there are paper piles in five areas of the house, there are dirty clothes spilling over washing baskets, the last two nights' dishes are still on the kitchen bench and dirty cups are sitting on the coffee table. Sound familiar?

 Develop a routine, pattern or 'ritual' that helps to keep things in order, and helps to keep you organised. Sticking to that routine is the key!

Harvesting spontaneity

Many people consider organised people to be boring. In fact, some disorganised people believe themselves to be spontaneous, creative, wild and exciting. Very often creative people may focus totally on their latest work of art, and this can be their excuse for being disorganised. It could be suggested that people whose lives depend on spontaneity more often than not live in a state of disorganisation. On the other hand, spontaneity can be a good thing if it means that you are able to deal with things on the spot. Handling tasks straight away is a spontaneous act that keeps your life flowing smoothly.

If you are unable to handle tasks as they arise, procrastinate about the tasks you have to do and don't set goals or plan ahead, you probably won't know how your life stands when you need to and this can present problems.

The consequences of disorganisation

Are you:

- regularly charged late fees for bills not paid on time? (*Wasting your money*)
- always losing things? (*Wasting your time looking for them and doubling the cost in having to replace them*)
- leaving less time for important things because you are constantly searching for possessions like keys, phone contacts and reading glasses? (*Wasting your time*)

💡   cooking three meals a night because your family or flat-mates arrive home at different times? (*Wasting your time, food and money*)

Self-inflicted chaos such as searching for keys, spending ten minutes looking for your reading glasses or leaving the washing up from a dinner party until the next night to clean up can eat up your valuable time.

Developing routines such as placing keys in the same place each time, hanging your reading glasses around your neck or washing up or stacking the dishwasher and switching it on before you go to bed will save you loads of time the next day. Small, simple tasks completed promptly become the cogs that keep the wheel of life turning efficiently.

Chronic clutterers or hoarders

How many times have we looked at an item of clothing hanging in our wardrobe, knowing that we haven't worn it in years. We say to ourselves, 'No, I can't throw that out. As soon as I do, I'm bound to want it for that special occasion.' So the item stays there, cluttering up the wardrobe, instead of being thrown out or given away. Most likely it is never worn. If the item of clothing were discarded there would be room for something new to come into our lives.

There are precious possessions that are given as gifts or handed down from generation to generation that shouldn't be discarded. It is natural instinct to want to treasure some of our belongings forever, but these items don't have to clutter up living spaces. Good organisers can carefully store things of sentimental value for the future.

For those of us whose parents grew up in the Depression, the urge to cling to our possessions is especially strong. We grew up with the ethos 'waste not, want not', so we are loath to discard possessions in case they may be valuable or useful later on.

It is important for us to understand the true value of the belongings we have accumulated. With some guidelines, however, we can be encouraged to look more dispassionately at our personal effects and make objective decisions about whether to keep these things close to hand, store or archive them for the future, or discard them. For those of us who hate waste, there are many worthwhile ways of disposing of items that are excess to requirements rather than simply throwing them in the bin.

Procrastinators

With the best of intentions and for a variety of reasons, we may postpone attempts at organising our lives or belongings, or begin the process but never seem to finish. There could be many reasons for the procrastination that results in cluttered environments or lives, including:

- preoccupation with a particular interest or creative pursuit
- lack of motivation
- a physical or mental disability
- perceiving that the task ahead is endless, 'so I won't start it'.

In most cases, those of us who procrastinate in organising our homes or businesses leave the clutter of the last task and can be unaffected by it. We would rather socialise with friends or watch television than get organised. There is always something better to do than the task of sorting out our lives.

The good news is that there is an end to the task of organising the garage or office. Once the task at hand is done — that is, categorised and organised — it's finished; and it will take a lot less time than you think.

Starting is the hardest part. It seems daunting to many, but once the process of streamlining has been done all that is left to do is maintenance.

People who fear change

Many of us feel safe within a particular routine or a familiar environment. We take comfort from continuity — from things remaining the same. We may be afraid of change. Our preference for routine and fear of change can prevent us from taking charge of our lives and overcoming our organisational problems.

Some of us fear that if we change a filing system or office layout we won't be able to find anything — we will lose control. We feel threatened by change so we make no attempt to get organised. We would rather continue doing what we've always done, even if it means remaining disorganised, rather than risk change and lack of control.

Busy people

Most people would agree that today there is so little time to enjoy the fruits of our labour. Juggling the running of our homes, maintaining a profitable career, raising children, having time with friends and family and allocating time for health and fitness — one wonders how we manage to cope with it all. Many people live for the weekend when they can have some 'time out', but usually much of this time is spent running children to sport commitments, doing the shopping and handling the things that don't get done during the week.

Sometimes things get out of hand — or out of order. We are so busy with so many commitments that the important task of organising our lives or our environment takes a low priority.

It is human nature to prioritise the things that are important to us — and time spent with our children or our partner, or at work, takes precedence over keeping the house in order. But organising our environment has to be faced sooner or later, and with some guidance it doesn't have to be as time-consuming as we imagine. With positive organisational skills we can find time on a regular basis to keep things in order, creating space for our higher priority commitments.

Learn to say no!

Some psychologists suggest that being disorganised can be an attention-seeking device. Being late means you make an entrance or being unprepared puts you in the spotlight. It may be a negative sort of attention seeking for some, but that's better than not being noticed at all. Being disorganised may be a way of rebelling, of not abiding by what authority tells you to do.

If your life is suffering because you can't say 'no' to anyone, then it's time to give back some time to you! If you say 'no', it doesn't mean that you are doing something wrong — it means you are taking control of your needs. A refusal backed up by a

clear and logical reason rarely offends anyone.

For example, perhaps you are consistently late for everything because you haven't planned ahead and you can't say no when you need to leave for an appointment. You are constantly apologising when you arrive and your friends or family are always (quietly) annoyed at being held up because of this.

Tight work deadlines may leave you stressed as you never plan ahead to meet timeframes. You take on more work than you can allocate time for and this causes conflict with co-workers and management. Stress becomes a part of how you live — you justify it by saying, 'I work better under pressure'. It doesn't cross your mind to overcome this conditioning by making an effort to plan ahead. By ignoring the signals and consistently working late into the night to complete work projects you are affecting your personal life.

Your lack of organisation doesn't just impact on you. All people and situations around you are also affected by your inability to be punctual.

Natural inclination versus learned behaviour

Many people are by nature organised. These people are logical, ordered or left-brain thinkers. Some of my clients are extremely organised and just use my service because I can help them stay that way.

At the other end of the scale are the people who don't think in logical ways but come up with great ideas like designing a spaceship or wrapping an island in plastic. These people are creative or right-brain thinkers. They have no time for order as they're too busy doing what they do best — creating.

While these natural inclinations are important, people may lack organisational skills because they were not as children given guidelines or direction on how to keep belongings in order or be punctual. Consequently, as adults they have no model to follow. Such disorganised lives can be chaotic, but people are often unaware of living any other way.

Did you know that life is easier if you are organised? Naturally organised people think ahead and plan ahead. We set ourselves tasks to do and go over in our minds what steps are required to complete the task.

Hiring contractors

Many of us have so many responsibilities that it can be very hard to manage our lives the way we wish. Our priorities have changed, with the majority of families needing two incomes to support them adequately. So where do we find the time to keep on top of everything? We can now hire contractors to assist us.

In recent years the list of services available for those who are cash-rich but time-poor has grown enormously. Those who can afford to pay can hire contractors to provide a wide range of services, including gardening, lawn mowing, handyman services, nanny services, childcare, cleaning, window cleaning, car washing, dog grooming and walking, house minding, and house styling.

When hiring a contractor it is always helpful to get a recommendation from family or friends. If you can't find a particular service this way, look in your local telephone directory. There is a 'Domestic Help Services' section in the *Yellow Pages*. Local newspapers will have a section in their 'classifieds' for home help services.

Tips when hiring a contractor

It is often hard to ensure that the person you hire to provide a service is going to be reliable and punctual. When you make an initial appointment, record it in your diary. Ask them to notify you, with plenty of warning, should a problem arise that prevents them meeting the appointment. Ask them for a written quote, and hold them to it. It is important when you are contracting any sort of service provider to have everything in writing.

Ensure that service providers or contractors you hire do not undertake any further work or use additional materials without first checking with you. In this way you will avoid being presented with an invoice greater than the agreed price. If you change your mind about any aspect of the work or have asked for additional work outside the original written quote, this will obviously affect the price of the job. It's a good idea to request revised quotes in writing.

Be organised. Schedule times in your diary or calendar for the whole year so you know when your service provider is coming. If you do this you won't have to remember to organise times with them.

It may suit you to provide a key to your home for convenience to the service provider if you are not going to be there when the service is expected. This is common practice today with service providers you have met and know you can trust. Alternatively you may choose to leave a key in a safe place for them. Such arrangements enable you to keep to agreed times rather than having to organise another appointment time for when you will be there. This will also keep you on top of all your tasks.

Good neighbours often look out for one another, so if you are expecting a service provider on a certain day, tell your neighbour about it. You can often rely on neighbours to keep an eye on your home and to report any people or behaviours that appear to be suspicious.

2 Simple ways to overcome disorganisation

> *Whatever you can do, or dream you can, begin it. Boldness has genius, power and magic in it! Begin it now!*
>
> Goethe

I grew up in a busy but organised family. My parents had six children, with my twin sister and me being the youngest of the pack. My sister and I have four older brothers, including another set of twins. There were six children all under the age of ten once my sister and I were born. One might be forgiven for thinking that my parents were crazy to have all those children; however, they said they just wanted a large family — and the Lord provided! We can be sure of one thing: the family kept my parents extraordinarily busy.

My father was a physicist and worked long hours, so my mother ruled the roost and kept our lives very organised in his absence. I can always remember my parents planning and organising together, ensuring that we had a good routine in our lives so we'd be ready for the next moment in history. They were very organised.

When I was a little girl I used to wonder why my father put out his spoon, knife, plate, cup and saucer before he went to bed at night, as they were never there in the morning when I got up. He used to rise at 5.00 a.m. so that he could start his day in peace — any peace was a blessing with six children in the house. Even now, as an elderly man, he still has the same routine. What I realised later on was that he was doing tasks at night so he could save time in the morning. Any 'spare' time in the morning meant more time for him. A small task like laying out crockery, cutlery and the toaster made everything ready and available for their purpose and saved Dad time in the morning.

Our clean school uniforms, totally in order and exactly as required, were always ready to put on in the mornings after breakfast. Apart from washing and cooking for eight every day, and caring for our cat, dog and bird, my mother was always attending our school parents and citizens meetings, doing school canteen duty, ferrying us around to our various hobbies and interests, keeping the home spick and span and maintaining the peace. My mother even found time to return to work when my sister and I went to primary school. What is more amazing is that we were always on time. There was never a mess in our home. Everything had a place and that's where it lived.

My father would say to us, 'Put things away where you found them when you've finished using them.' I must have heard this a million times growing up, as we know parents often have to repeat themselves! One can only imagine how he felt having to repeat himself so often to six of us. But somehow the message sank in.

My parents were naturally organised. Even so, I have often wondered how they managed to keep everything running so smoothly. The key was to abide by some simple rules: plan ahead, maintain a routine and allocate a place for everything.

It's the small things that count

Complete small tasks as they arise rather than leaving them until later, when they may become much greater and more time-consuming. Alternatively, write them on a list. This will ensure that they won't stay in your mind and will free you up to do other things.

You'll be amazed at how little time some tasks take to do. We tend to blow timeframes out of proportion, as there always seems so much to do. Become aware of times where you could be doing something, any little thing, to keep your life in order, to save you time in the future.

Take note of your life and its processes over a period of one week, being mindful of times when things are obviously out of control. Write a list of small tasks that could become routines in your new life on the road to becoming organised.

Embracing change

Change can be daunting for some, but if we see change as a challenge, to be achieved and rewarded, then making the change can be less painful.

Most of us at some time in our lives have the deep desire to do something different. It could be to:

- resign from our job
- learn to play a musical instrument
- take up art classes
- move house.

Whatever it may be, we feel that innate desire stirring within us to do something different. We may be fed up with living the way we've been going about our lives. We know in ourselves that we are looking for a change and will not be the same again because of that realisation. Our desire will not go away until we deal with it.

The urge for change or to change the way we do things will keep occurring in our lives, more frequently for some, less frequently for others. We may choose to ignore it and justify rationally why we can't do it or why we don't have the time. But the yearning will remain. That's what change is and it results in that exciting feeling in the pit of our stomachs. It's not enough for someone else to tell us to change. We have to want change ourselves and we have to have the motivation to make our lives change in the way we would like.

If you've had this feeling about getting yourself organised, then you're halfway there. There's only one more step to take, and that's just to start anywhere. It doesn't matter where. The results you will gain after an organising session will far outweigh the heaviness you must feel carrying around the constant reminder that things are out of control or lacking order in your life. A weight will be lifted off your shoulders. The completed task in front of you will also give you loads of confidence and you will feel strengthened and invigorated having achieved it.

Clients often say to me after we've finished a task that they feel relieved, excited, elated, lighter, clearer, fulfilled, happy and proud — all wonderful feelings to experience, I say. That's the added bonus for getting organised — we feel great afterwards! What more could we ask for?

The support of a buddy

Not everyone has access to a service like mine. The next best thing is to enlist the assistance of a friend or relative who can help with the sorting process. When finishing a job with a client, I have often heard the comment, 'I could have done this.' Clients know they could have done what I have done for them because the task *is* relatively easy. It can just look daunting.

Sometimes when we're alone we just don't know where to begin. We can become overwhelmed by the task at hand and crave an objective eye to help us put our lives and the tasks we need to do back in perspective. Most of us enjoy having someone there with us, cheering us on, supporting us while we complete the task. It can be so much easier to do a job when there is an extra pair of hands available or when someone is there to guide us. Often it's good just having someone standing by to help us face whatever may be discovered or uncovered during the sifting process.

The criteria of a good buddy

- You are a motivated person and love giving of yourself and helping people.
- You love a challenge.
- You are able to assist physically and mentally.
- You are a logical thinker and also love being creative.
- You can follow through and complete tasks.
- You have time to help or are willing to allocate some of your time.

Steps to enlisting the help of a buddy

- Step 1: Telephone or email a friend or relative who you know will *want* to help you out.
- Step 2: Explain that you need some help in sorting out your life and tell them what you need to do.
- Step 3: Plan a time (for example, a two-hour or four-hour period) as soon as possible and schedule it into your diary.
- Step 4: Stick to the plan. Let nothing distract you.

Another option is to exchange some time with a friend. You can help them de-clutter or sort out an area of their life one day and then diarise another time for them to help you. With two working on the project, you both benefit and get things achieved in a smaller amount of time.

Setting up routines

There is no 'absolute truth' that forms the foundations of organisation. Everyone is an individual, therefore it is most important to have a system or routine that will work for you.

Think about the things in your life that need to be done regularly, then set a plan for when you will do them and how. For instance, washing up after cooking is part of your food preparation routine. Cleaning down the kitchen benches and putting things away once all the ingredients have been used is another part. After eating, the next step is cleaning up —

washing the dishes or stacking the dishwasher and wiping down the benches and sinks ready for the next meal or snack. If you stick to this routine you will save time and have one less thing to think about later on.

Now choose a routine that is important in your life. It can be any routine — just start somewhere! Write down the steps that it will take to complete the routine.

Some people forget to take the washing out of the machine when it is finished and it may stay there for hours or days wet. When the washing is finally removed it smells mouldy and has to be washed again.

Keep focused on what you are trying to accomplish. You should generally be able to handle a few tasks at any one time. If you get interrupted at any stage through the process or routine, that's OK as long as you go back to what you were doing and complete it before you move on to the next task.

Apply the following formula to any routine that you want to establish.

DOING THE WASHING

Collect soiled clothes.

Separate light, coloured and dark clothing.

Place the washing in the washing machine.

Add detergent, set the control function to wash cycle and start the machine.

Once the load is finished, hang the clothes out to dry or put them in the clothes dryer.

Bring the clothes in from the line when they are dry or remove them from the dryer.

Fold the clothes and put them away.

How to set up a routine

1 Make the decision to start a routine
2 Decide clearly on the routine you want to start.
3 Choose a time to start — it could be right now!
4 Write down the plan on paper.
5 Put a time in your diary to carry out your plan, or do it now, following the steps you have set out on paper.

Folding clothes straight off the line or as soon as the dryer is finished can save you time. The longer clothes sit in the dryer or the clothes basket dry but unfolded, the more chance there is that they'll become wrinkled and that you'll have to iron them before you wear them.

Make a plan to put on a load of washing before you eat breakfast each day, or two or three times a week. Make sure you undertake this task at the same time each time. Once breakfast is finished, the load should be ready to hang out to dry. This saves you having to wait for the load to finish. By setting the timeframe for doing the task it becomes a routine.

Positive thinking

Routines like brushing your teeth before bed or after breakfast can blend with your life after a while and become second nature to you. Once you establish a routine for tasks, you will find that you automatically complete them at set times.

If it helps, write down or type out the steps you need to take to accomplish your tasks. If you do this, you won't have to think about what needs to be done in what order, as you will have the steps within easy reach.

I believe in the power of positive thinking, and replacing negative thoughts with good ones. Having positive words to assist you in the process of organising yourself can be likened to having support to help you feel inspired to achieve the outcome. Inject your thoughts with positive words — affirmations to uplift and enhance how you feel about the task ahead to align the mind with the action or activity you are about to undertake.

A routine affirmation for success

Try doing the following affirmation or 'mantra for success' for one week, religiously, and see what happens. The types of changes you can expect after one week are that you may feel more positive about the changes you are about to make. You may also feel excited about the process rather than feeling indifferent or rejecting the idea entirely. You could also find yourself being more organised as a whole, because you have been reinforcing your mind with positive, affirmative words rather than negative thoughts about the process. Subconsciously this shifts the way you think about the idea.

You've made the decision to do it now, so sit down and stay still for five minutes and concentrate on listening to your intuition about organising and doing the routine chosen for a whole week. What you may find are feelings of excitement, happiness, being relaxed, being in control, and relief. You may also feel a tug in the pit of your stomach making you feel full of dread, fearful or blocked. Just continue to inject good thoughts into your mind about what you want to do, and tap into the feeling of 'knowing' that it will benefit you to be more organised. Think about the positives.

Make up a positive phrase to reflect exactly what it is you want to achieve. You could say to yourself one of the following:

'I know I'm ready to begin this now!'

'I feel complete and fulfilled now that I have my life in order!'

'I am now open and willing to allow myself to take this step forward — to become organised.'

'I am now totally organised in every area of my life.'

If you find this is silly or difficult, just say it aloud in front of a mirror and see how you feel. You may feel confronted with this process at first, but just continue. Keep saying it over and over. You could plan to say it one hundred times a day to begin with, while you are on your way to work, going for a walk or cooking a meal.

Write the chosen phrase down on some coloured board or paper. This is your mantra for the week. Stick it on a mirror, the front cover of your diary or your noticeboard. Wherever you put it, be sure it is somewhere that you frequent so you will read it over and over. You can use it for however long you wish; a week is a good start. Change it the following week to another one.

Notice what happens over the following week. It will encourage you to be excited about becoming organised.

Take care not to clutter other people's lives

On a number of occasions when parents of young children visit friends, they let the children 'run riot' in someone else's home. In other words, they don't give any direction when it is needed. The children often upturn anything they can get their hands on, or spill drinks or food on carpets and toys. Meanwhile, the parents sit calmly, sipping coffee and continuing in deep conversation with their friends, without appearing to notice their child's path of destruction. Does this sound like a familiar scene?

I can understand that there are certain times when it's necessary or unavoidable to block out everything around you. Perhaps it may be the parent's own time-out. Whatever the case, when it's time to go they often get up as if nothing has happened around them and go home — leaving the place in chaos.

Keep yourself and your family in check when visiting people. Try to leave the place just how it was when you walked in. If your child spills a drink, wipe it up. If they upturn the bookcase, put the books back where they belong for the owner. Your friends don't need more work when you leave. Help them wash up or stack the dishwasher before you leave and consider the effort that has already gone into having you there in the first place. Ask your children to help your friend's children put away the toys and playthings when they have finished playing.

When minding a person's home or staying with friends, leave the place in the same condition it was in when you arrived — or better. A good visitor can leave a place in such a way that it looks like they've never been there.

The stars do it — so do as they do!

You can't help but wonder how movie stars keep track of all their clothes and possessions — especially when you read about their shopping sprees. Most stars would hire personal assistants to help them manage their lives, so they have the assistance whenever they need to de-clutter. The following question was put to a number of high-profile people and the answers were published in the 'Star Talk' section of Who Weekly, May 2001.

Question: When was the last time you cleared out your closet and what did you discard?

Minnie Driver: *'Three weeks ago, and I threw out everything I haven't worn in the past three years. I think I even threw out some cashmere sweaters.'*

Moby: *'Once a month I go through my closet. When I do photo shoots people give me clothes that I know I am never going to wear again.'*

Gena Lee Nolin: *'Three weeks ago. I threw out 20 pairs of shoes. I'm a shoe-aholic. They went to charity.'*

The lucky people who shop at charity and recycled fashion shops in Hollywood, I say! Take a leaf from these celebrities' books and clear out your wardrobe regularly.

3 Time management

Brian Tracy, a US motivational speaker and time management authority, has produced a series of tapes on time management called 'How to Master Your Time'. One of the key points he makes is that 'no-one is born with the gene that automatically gives you the ability to be organised and similarly no-one is born with the gene that dictates you will be disorganised'. This is very true. Organisational skills are learned traits and anyone can develop them. Even if you allow your organisational skills to lapse into disuse, they are easily enough relearned.

When trying to save time running your life and everything that this encompasses, you need to break tasks down into manageable chunks, otherwise the big picture will be frightening.

Go easy on yourself to begin with and set achievable goals. Try not to be daunted by the big picture. There is a way to handle every situation we are presented with, and that includes organising our time and organising ourselves.

Discipline means having an action or task in mind, and planning when you'll do it. Discipline is the first mind-set you must develop to be organised. Staying organised means managing your time accordingly. Time management is basically setting goals, applying discipline, and planning when and how you'll achieve your goals.

Setting goals

Just for something completely different, embrace the opportunity to clean out a cupboard or the garage. Take it on as a challenge. Set a goal to do it. Plan a time — perhaps a Saturday afternoon. You could say to yourself, 'If I clean my garage today, what will I find?' If you haven't looked among the boxes and piles for years, you might have forgotten what you have there; you never know what might be hidden just waiting for you to reclaim. You could find something of value that could be sold. Setting goals like this is the way to master lack of discipline, procrastination and chronic laziness. Start enjoying the challenge.

Personally, I love a challenge. When I go into a client's

home or office and see the task in front of me, it really doesn't daunt me in the slightest. It could make me sick at the thought of the job ahead, but it's just the way you treat the situation. I see it as a process to be worked through — it's about attitude. See it as a new adventure or a new phase of your life about to begin and it will be less onerous.

Our minds can play funny tricks on us when we view a stack of clutter on a bench. We may think that it looks all too hard to tackle because it will take ages to sort through it. It is human nature to postpone unpleasant tasks. The truth is that it may only take thirty minutes or an hour and then it's done. Once we realise how little time it has taken, we may say, 'I could have done this ages ago!'

Once I was contracted by a large organisation to help with streamlining the flow of work in the office and work with staff, one-to-one at their workstations and desks. The goal was to remove clutter, create a place for everything 'to live', cut down on double-handling of information, create procedures for tasks, and stock the office efficiently and stylishly.

Many of the staff had piles of paperwork in their in-trays. Many of these people had become overwhelmed, gradually watching their piles of paper grow larger and larger each day. In most cases they had prioritised all the items in their in-trays, but the problem was that the low-priority tasks were not getting handled and they also seemed to be multiplying.

I asked them to go through their in-trays to ascertain how long they thought these tasks would take to complete. As they went through the papers, they stuck yellow Post-it notes on the top of each and wrote on the note how long they thought the task would take.

When this was finished, most seemed amazed that a lot of the tasks would take under ten minutes to complete. By grouping the tasks in order of how long the task would take, they could see how it might be possible to fit these tasks into their busy day. I suggested that when they had a spare half an hour (for example, if a meeting was cancelled or rescheduled) they could fit some of these 'in-tray' items into their day and complete them.

Some objected, saying they never got any free time. They are doing the jobs of two or three people, so how could they fit it in? The only solution I could suggest was to schedule in a time to accomplish the tasks. On arrival each day they could schedule in a 'meeting' with themselves for half an hour or one hour so they had the time to complete the work.

You must have the big picture in sight, but break tasks down into smaller, manageable tasks.

It's hard to put a timeframe on doing a task like tidying up the garden. The time it will take depends on how long it has been since it's been tidied and what state it's in. Some of us have well-maintained gardens that have got a bit messy, so it shouldn't take us more than an hour to tidy up. (Of course, in most cases this one-hour timeframe wouldn't include maintaining the garden as well.) You can get a lot done in this time, including tidying up verandahs and outdoor living areas.

In your diary, block out time to do this. Put a timeframe around the next task you want to achieve and book it into your diary too. Once you've completed these tasks, you'll see very quickly that your time has been well spent.

Planning ahead

Our lives are never in a state of perfection. In fact, I don't believe that perfection is possible. In this ever-changing world there is always something that we need to change or adjust or just something else we want to do. We all wish we could be perfect but we're all only human and with this comes human failings. It's impossible to be perfect so don't even try.

No one can be totally organised all the time. It's impossible to have everything — our whole life and what it encompasses — exactly where we want it at the same time or the right time. We are entitled to give ourselves a break — I know

I have on some occasions. By all means leave things out of order from time to time, but have a plan to sort things out in the near future.

Planning ahead is the key to organisation. Once you plan, you take away the worry. You can relax once you have planned to tackle something that has really been bothering you or that you need to get done.

Plan to set a goal to de-clutter the bathroom cabinet next Sunday evening to start off the week on a fresh note. The task will probably only take an hour at the most — try it.

Time management tips

 Always have a pen and a notebook beside the phone to take messages. Take the message details and record the date, the time of the call and who it's for. (Personally, I like to use a journal to write messages in, because I like to keep a permanent record of my messages in case I need to refer to it later.) Avoid using loose paper: it can look untidy or get lost.

 Schedule in manageable times to organise one section of the house or office. Breaking the task of organisation into small chunks enables you to complete the task relatively quickly and gain a sense of achievement. (For example, break the task into rooms, then areas within rooms. Write a list of the areas you wish to work on.)

Completing one area will encourage and motivate you to move on to the next.

Try to group 'like' tasks together. For example, if you have a number of telephone calls to make, do them all in succession, jotting down on the relevant paperwork the time of the call, the date and who you spoke to.

Have something extra to do next to you while making telephone calls. Calls sometimes take longer than anticipated, and while waiting you can be reading short articles such as your child's school newsletter or the latest investment report from your broker, or planning in your diary for the next week.

When breaking tasks down into blocks of time, schedule the block of time into your diary or calendar. Then follow through by doing the task you planned, if possible allowing nothing to distract you. This will help you to keep your life running smoothly and to achieve the things you want.

Completion

Completion is the key to good organising skills — and it will save you time. Discipline yourself to finish what you start. Get into the habit of putting things away when you've finished using them. This is a discipline I learned as a very small child and have lived with all my life. I have made a habit of tidying up after myself and I believe this saves me a lot of collective task-time.

Interruptions can and do occur, especially when young children are around, but you can always pick up a task where you left off or put it away until there is a more suitable time to complete it. Write a note if you need to remind yourself of where you are up to with the task, then you won't have to think about it when you get back to it.

To make sure you complete tasks, set achievable goals. By setting achievable goals and planning up front how you will complete each task, you will become better organised and create time for the more important things in your life.

Select a task — any task, big or small. It could be cleaning out your desk drawers or creating more space in the linen press. Then write down the task on a piece of paper. For example: You have just successfully de-cluttered your consciousness as well, as you now have one less task to think about.

CLEAN OUT THE LINEN PRESS

Write down step-by-step the necessary steps to complete that task. For example:

1. Take everything out of the linen press.

2. Clean the shelves of the linen press.

3. Sort through the linen and decide which items should be retained and which items can be discarded.

4. Neatly fold the linen that will be retained.

5. Stack everything into the linen press in groups - hand towels in one pile, bath towels together, bathmats together etc. - ensuring that the most frequently used items are placed on the most accessible shelves

4 Time-saving life skills

> *There's a way to do it better ... FIND IT!*
>
> Thomas Edison

Taking care of household paperwork

Piles of household paperwork represent postponed decision-making. Aim to sort papers frequently and to complete sorting before the next pile begins.

Allow time for handling the paperwork associated with running your home. Allocate one or two hours in your diary per week. It may be an evening during the week or a Saturday morning when you say 'no' to everything else to make the time to maintain your paperwork. Doing so will lighten the load. It may take a combination of discipline, focus and practice to start with, but if you stick to the routine, sooner or later it will become automatic.

Your allocated time is decision time. By focusing this time

specifically on paying household bills, making phone calls, running errands, buying gifts, organising social gatherings, planning your children's commitments or keeping on top of home projects (such as organising tradespeople for a task), you will be able to keep on top of the paper and projects.

How to keep a 'things to do' list

 In the time leading up to your scheduled time for a task, write a list of 'things to do' and keep it in a spiral or loose-leaf notebook (loose pages can be lost easily). When your scheduled time arrives, your list will be ready, so you will avoid wasting time having to think about what needs to be done and can get the most out of the time you have allocated.

 Keep adding to your list regularly throughout the week. Keep your 'things to do' book in an easy-to-find location near your telephone area or home office desk drawer, or allocate a file in your filing cabinet and label it 'House'.

 Cross items off your 'things to do' list as you do them. This will prove to be extremely rewarding. You will experience a sense of control and feel less stressed because your time has been productive. You will also feel that your goal of having your life in order can work. Stick to this routine and you will see how everything will begin to flow.

Pat yourself on the back. You've achieved your goal! Reward yourself. Take time to have lunch with a friend, play a round of golf or take your partner out for dinner.

 If in the beginning you run overtime and haven't completed everything on your list, don't wait another week — schedule another hour into the same week. Do the unfinished tasks then. This way you won't be overburdened or late with tasks the following week.

Diary action plan

- Prepare your 'things to do' the day before or as appointments arise. It shouldn't take you more than five minutes to do this each day.

- Schedule in times for things you need to do, allowing enough travelling time and time to complete tasks on your way to appointments.

- Keep your eye on the time. Keep your list or diary available to refer to if in doubt.

- Most importantly, keep your word. If you say you are going to be somewhere at a certain time, make sure it happens. Hold-ups happen, so if you are going to be late to an appointment, telephone the person and let them know. (When I am working with a client, I try to arrive five

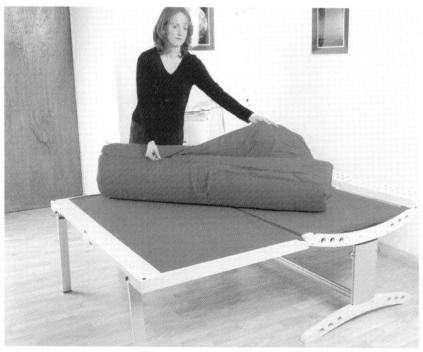

The Besk: a table or desk by day, a double-bed at night.

From top left, clockwise: Freedom Furniture Bucco Boxes, Kubico drawers, Pandanus baskets, Sempurut laundry baskets and Monash Robe.

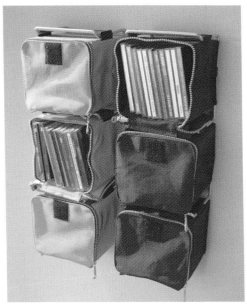

From top left, clockwise: Ikea multilevel storage bin, CD storage bags, shelves and assorted boxes.

Assorted stationery from kikki.K.

or ten minutes early to allow myself time to touch-up my make-up and to take my time walking in. I try to always be on time — not early, not late.)

 Tick tasks off as you complete them.

If you reach a destination early, you can purposely time your arrival to be perfectly on time, every time.

How to save time with your 'reading' pile of newspapers and magazines

Don't overburden yourself with keeping a 'to read' pile of unnecessary information that you know you'll never get to. It places extra stress on you, so follow the tips below to free up the time you would normally take on reading newsworthy information.

 When reading the weekend newspapers, break the paper down as soon as it arrives into 'must read' and 'discard' piles.

 Discard irrelevant sections or sections of no interest to you. (For instance, if you're not in the market for a new or used car and not looking for employment, throw these sections away immediately.)

 Read the news summary section.

- Set aside feature articles of interest to read in the evening in front of the television, while waiting on the telephone or while travelling on public transport.

- Make 'executive' decisions about what you will read and what is simply not important. This physical de-cluttering of the newspaper will sub-consciously relieve the stress of having too much to read, and you can ensure that you read the pertinent things in your life more quickly.

- When reading new magazines, mark the page for later reading or cut out the articles of interest for filing. This way you can go back to the magazine when you have the time to consume the information or will know where to locate the information when you need it.

- When reading business magazines and the like, avoid the stress of thinking that the magazine must be read cover to cover.

- Arrange to have the newspapers you <u>must</u> read delivered. This saves you time stopping off at the shop or leaving the house on the weekends to get them.

Time-saving 'things to do' when waiting for the dinner to cook

- Add items to your shopping list.
- Feed the animals and wash their used plates.

- Fill the kettle ready to make a cup of tea.
- Take out any recycling waste.
- Stack the dishwasher or wash up any dirty dishes.
- Clean up the kitchen.
- Switch on the water sprinkler system or water the garden.
- Prepare lunches for the following day.
- Remove leftovers from the refrigerator.
- Put on a load of washing.
- Unpack the shopping.
- Transfer food into storage containers.

Time-saving 'things to do' when watching television

- Arrange photographs in albums or photo storage boxes.
- Read short articles from magazines and newspapers.
- Ride an exercise bike.
- Do sewing repairs such as sewing on buttons or taking up hems.
- Make or review 'to do' lists.
- Pay bills.
- Give yourself a manicure.
- Choose gift ideas from catalogues.
- Fold the washing.
- Do the ironing.

Commonsense time-saving ideas

The secret to keeping organised is to do as many small tasks as you can while you wait for other things to be done, like cooking or doing the washing.

Plug in your mobile phone for charging, wash a few dishes and pull out the ingredients for dinner all in the time it takes to boil the water for a cup of tea. While your tea is brewing, you can cut up the vegetables, wash the rice and prepare it for cooking. Now you can have your tea (timeframe — five minutes)! Then, when dinner is cooking, check your e-mails, read your mail, make some quick phone calls and then sit down to relax over a great meal. Of course, this depends what you are cooking, but many meals take approximately thirty minutes to cook.

When walking from one room to another, or from one end of the house to the other, collect things that 'live' in another room or area, and put them away where they belong as you go. If you constantly do this you'll find few things will be left lying around.

If you have a staircase in your home, leave things that don't live downstairs at the bottom of the staircase. Train your family or flatmates to take their possessions with them when they go up the stairs and put them back where they belong.

☼ If you or your family, circle of friends or business contacts move house or premises regularly, keeping up-to-date with their address changes is an ongoing task. Very often when you get a new address the postcode may be missing. When you have organised to look up a postcode to complete addressing an envelope for a birthday, Christmas or anniversary card, don't forget to update your address book with the new postcode at the same time. This will save you having to look it up again.

Unfortunately, tasks that aren't completed stay on our minds until we handle them. Once they're done we have one less thing to think about. So do things as you think of them and your 'things to do' list will not get overwhelming.

Moving from a big house to a small flat

'I have just divorced after thirty years of marriage and moved from a large house into a small flat. I need some help organising my flat and sorting through my things.' — Kay, early sixties, retired professional, traveller.

Kay moved into her flat six months ago but hasn't yet been able to get organised. She has piles of papers and memorabilia in every room. She is not effectively utilising the limited storage space she has. Kay wants to take stock of what she has and create a space for everything.

The first place to start is the piles of papers, many of which haven't been looked at for years. Much to our surprise and delight we find an investment certificate for $50,000 hidden among the papers — an investment Kay has long forgotten she made.

We sort through the paperwork and create files for banking, contacts, interesting articles, investments, legal issues, properties and travel. Kay is currently engaged in a property settlement court case. We create specific files for the paperwork associated with this as well as for keeping a clear record of communications between the parties concerned.

Next we tackle Kay's storage problems. I do a survey to establish what storage facilities exist and to identify opportunities to take maximum advantage of them. We sort items of memorabilia into those she definitely wants to keep and those she can cull. Kay has multiples of many things such as kitchen utensils and cooking equipment and collects lots of memorabilia on her travels. She purchases plastic storage bins to store those things that are of sentimental value but seldom used. Items that she wishes to access more regularly are stored in a cupboard in her spare room. I prepare an inventory of what is contained in the storage bins so that Kay knows exactly what she has in her home.

Kay rings me a number of times following our organisation session to thank me, especially for helping her rediscover her lost investment. Kay also points out how much easier it is to participate in the court case now she has the confidence of knowing that the files she takes to court have everything in order. This gives her a feeling of control and helps her succeed in court.

5 Eight steps to getting organised

Action is what counts. Otherwise Nike's slogan would be 'Just say it.'

Anon

When getting organised it's important to remember to be brave. Face clutter fearlessly, for you are inviting change and transformation to occur. The more we discard of the old, the more space we make for the new. You will need to be prepared to make decisions about your possessions.

Once you have decided which space you wish to organise, take the following steps.

The eight steps

1 Get prepared!

Find a large garbage bag and at least four cardboard boxes. The garbage bag is for throwing away or recycling clothes or linen. (You may need more than one!) The boxes are to be used as follows:

- Box 1 is for paper recycling.

- Box 2 is for plastic or glass items or hard objects to be recycled.

- Box 3 is for plastic or glass items or hard objects to be given away (to family, friends or ex-lovers).

- Box 4 is for items to be thrown away (or taken to the tip).

Note that you can collect empty boxes from your local supermarket or fruit and vegetable shop.

2 Get started!

Choose a room or area that has been annoying you. Walk in, take a deep, enthusiastic breath and off you go! The aim here is to create a 'place for everything' to live. Start anywhere. Of course you can plan your attack to a certain degree by selecting an area that you really need to sort out right now — like an office desk, a kitchen cupboard or a chest of drawers.

3 Get clear!

Take everything out of the cupboard or drawers — and I mean everything — and place the contents on the floor.

4 Get listing!

Take a piece of paper and a pen and write down anything that needs to be actioned — a 'things to do' list. Keep items separately on the floor or place them in plastic bags or containers with a note saying what they are. (Writing this down reinforces future planning and saves you relying on your memory.)

5 Get decisive!

Clean the cupboard or drawer surfaces thoroughly. While waiting for the surfaces to dry, start sifting through your possessions. Keep progressing gently, deciding what you'd like to keep and what you don't like or need any more. As you are sorting through your belongings you should bear the following key questions in mind:

- Do I *absolutely* love it?

- Do I *still* need it?

- Does it support who I am now in my life?

- What thoughts (*positive and/or negative*), memories or emotions do I associate with it?

- Does it need to be fixed or repaired and am I willing to do this now?

- If it's time to let it go, am I going to sell it or give it away, and when?

6 Get actioning!

If the object doesn't work or is damaged, decide on the spot whether it can be fixed relatively easily or whether you want to bother. If you say yes to either question, put the object into an 'action' pile at the side of a room and add it to the 'things to do' list. If you decide not to do anything with the object, put it into one of the boxes in step 1.

A home that needs de-cluttering

'I live by myself and need some organising done around my home.' — Bill, mid-fifties, divorced, professional, manager of multinational company.

Bill needs help organising tasks around the home such as carpet cleaning, garden maintenance, completing a half-built laundry, sorting personal paperwork and culling clutter. He has been divorced for a number of years and has been used to his wife handling these tasks. He doesn't have the time during working hours to organise tradespeople to attend to tasks and complete projects for him, so many tasks have been left to the point where the whole house is seriously in need of attention.

Bill's children, all in their twenties, have left home, although their bedrooms appear to be inhabited; it is as though they still live there. Cupboards are spilling with old clothes and outdated toys and many other items that are not needed any longer. Bill wants the bedrooms to be sorted out too, as well as the boxes of 'stuff' that are piling up in the hallways and rooms and making it difficult to walk inside the front door.

The first thing we do is to prioritise the most important aspects of this project. Bill wants to have an efficient filing system to keep all his regular 'home' paperwork, and he wants to have quotes organised to complete the renovation of the laundry, to have the carpet cleaned and to maintain the garden.

As Bill is not at home while I am working, I am able to supervise all tradespeople and put into action many things for him while he is working. I establish a new filing system by sorting through and categorising all paperwork found in three drawers. I find bank account books with thousands of dollars in them among the papers — money that Bill was unaware he had. I organise a gardener to mow the lawns and tidy up the trees and shrubs, and carpet cleaners to clean the carpets in the whole house. I sort out cupboards, resulting in many things being culled.

During this process I give Bill 'homework' to action at night. He has to make daily decisions to keep the process rolling, and becomes excited that the pressure is easing. Day by day he can see the number of tasks decreasing in size and he feels happier coming home to a house that is organised.

After three weeks, Bill is able to come home to a house that he can live in more easily without having to be constantly reminded of tasks he should be doing. The front and back gardens are tidy and very presentable. His carpets are clean, the hallways and cupboards are organised and more spacious, and Bill now has a filing system to work with. He says he wants to keep it this way now that it is in order, and is determined to do this.

7 Get categorising!

Separate items into groups or categories. For instance, if it's paperwork that you are sorting through, set up simple categories for everything, such as Car, Children's information (making a category for each child's name), Correspondence (Personal), Correspondence (Business), Health, Home (renovations, purchases etc.), Insurance, Investments (share certificates, etc.) and Tax.

8 Get creative!

Now that the sorting has been done, you can start putting things back where they belong. If you didn't have a place for everything, create areas or sections by grouping like items. Try to place things carefully so that you can see everything on the shelf, arranging taller items at the back and smaller ones at the front. Label jars to make the contents clear.

When sorting through any storage area, remember that in most cases you only need one of everything, so give the rest away to a charity or friends. Items broken, chipped or stained are not what you want in your life. They can be easily replaced and you probably don't enjoy using them anyway. Likewise with the linen press — throw away those torn or stained tea-towels or pillowslips and sheets. Let them go! If it's a paper-work system you need to establish, see chapter 20.

If you have a problem letting go of anything, practise saying to yourself, 'Something new is going to come into my life now.' It would be interesting to take note of replacements that come into your life for things you have decided to part with. It may come from a family member or a friend wanting to 'off-load' some personal belongings! Magic happens ...

Admire your efforts. Pat yourself on the back! Not only do you have more space, but you will now save time when looking for an item and you will find it with ease.

Part Two
Organising your home

6 First impressions

> *In order to seek one's own direction, one must simplify the mechanics of ordinary, everyday life.*
>
> Plato

First impressions will often influence the attitude of first-time visitors to our homes. Think about how it feels when you walk into a home that is dusty, dirty and untidy. It looks like the occupants are really busy — too busy in fact to pay any attention to the way they are living. You don't know where to sit as the lounge is covered with books and clothes and maybe even last night's dinner plates, and you have to step over an array of toys to move around the room. Messy environments provide excess stimulation to the brain, which can be distracting.

Now think about how you feel when you walk into a home that is pristine, tidy and organised. For me it's a real pleasure to be in surroundings that have order. You are able to think more clearly if you have a clear and well-ordered space and you can admire your surroundings and appreciate the qualities around you.

Sometimes we subconsciously 'label' people either organised or disorganised, motivated or lazy, proud or uninterested. Many of us would automatically make a negative judgement about people who live in a disorganised house. Some people would make a negative judgement about the people who live in the ordered house too, saying, 'they mustn't have too much to do in their lives' or 'they don't have kids'.

How we live is certainly a choice in life. If we decide we don't like the way our home presents and want to change it, this is a positive change to make. We can be sure we'll gain respect from friends and family and people will notice the changes.

Organising the outside of your home

Visiting a new property can give you great insight into the mind-space of the occupants. Sometimes you may see gardens overgrown and front entrances strewn with shoes, toys, cartons of newspapers and bottles and cans — a real mess. Not good feng shui, the experts tell us!

Other times you will come across perfectly manicured gardens and entrances that are neat and orderly. Fragrant aromas abound and there is a feeling of calm. There's nothing like entering your front garden and loving the look of it, feeling satisfied and comfortable that it presents the way you want it to.

Tips for enhancing the presentation of the outside of your home

- *Keep garbage bins out of sight. If there is nowhere to do this, you could build or have built a simple box or screen for them to sit behind. You can place pot plants or plant shrubs to disguise the area in front of them. Get creative!*

- *Trim shrubs and branches to work in with the flow of your pathway and entrance to create ambience. Decorate with fairy lights and lanterns holding candles to create a magical invitation for your visitors.*

- *Keep paths swept, especially if you have leaves or flowers dropping from trees as these can become slippery in wet weather and a hazard for visitors. These days, people are quick to sue for physical damage resulting in negligence anywhere — on the footpath, in the supermarket, wherever. The last thing you need is to be sued by someone who slipped over on wet leaves or flowers on your garden path.*

Do a general tidy-up outside each week or whenever you see the need. Don't let things get too out of hand. You don't want to have to race around tidying up outside the house when visitors are due.

Train your children to place their shoes neatly at the door and to hang their coats on designated hooks.

If you own animals, place food and water bowls in an area that is out of the way of doorways and pathways. Keep the area clean.

Hang your hose neatly over the tap or roll it up around a hose-wheel. You don't want visitors tripping over it on their way into your home.

Organise a gardener to come every month to keep your garden in order and looking its best. This takes the burden off your shoulders and everything will be maintained on a regular basis. You will have more time to do the things you would rather do.

7   Kitchens and pantries

Kitchens

One of the most important rooms in the house, the kitchen is usually the hive of home activity. Therefore it makes sense to ensure that it is a place of order and cleanliness and that you have the things you need to use at your fingertips. Everything you use in your kitchen should have 'a home'. By implementing certain routines it will be easier to keep this room organised.

Firstly, de-clutter each cupboard and storage space. Throw away broken or chipped crockery, and recycle bowls, plates and platters that you don't like or use. Don't limit yourselves to just these items æ throw away anything that doesn't work. If the item is something that you still love or has sentimental value, arrange to have it fixed.

Group like items together such as storage containers, crockery, utensils, food items, cutlery, even things like tea-towels, placemats and tablecloths. It is a good idea to ensure that kitchen items are stored as close as possible to the work area in which they are regularly used. Storing your kitchen utensils so that they are convenient to your work areas can be tricky, depending on the space available. For example, try to have utensils within handy reach of the cooking area; and keep tea, coffee, mugs and sugar near where the kettle is boiled.

If you don't have much storage space in your kitchen and you can't change it at this time, purchase stand-alone shelving from furniture or homeware shops to extend your kitchen storage areas. Baskets of all shapes, sizes and colours can also provide further storage spaces.

Hanging pots and pans from a ceiling frame has become a popular alternative to storing them in cupboards. They look decorative and give your kitchen a country or French feel. (If these items are not used regularly, they will need to be dusted and cleaned to maintain their appeal.)

Utilise unused wall space by mounting electrical appliances such as microwave ovens on brackets affixed to walls. This will save your much-needed bench space. Make sure the microwave oven is mounted at the appropriate height for everyone using it.

When designing a new kitchen, take all the items that will live there into account, arranging the cupboards and shelving accordingly. Make your drawers and shelves roomy. You can never have too much storage space.

Kitchen tips

- *Ensure that counter tops are kept clean and clutter-free by putting away items you don't use regularly.*

- *Make sure you have uncluttered bench spaces to work on when preparing food.*

- *Keep all kitchen appliance instruction booklets and warranties stored together in a drawer or in a manilla folder in your pantry.*

- *Use large woven baskets for storing pastry tins and cake tins under counter tops. Set up an area for rubbish and recycling, but keep it out of sight. Hide your waste bins by mounting them inside cupboard doors. Establish a compost bin or area in your backyard to allow you to recycle your food wastes. Do this daily.*

- *Use a wire or plastic rack or a bowl for storing citrus fruits, onions and potatoes to ensure air-flow. This will inhibit mould growth.*

Pantries

The pantry is my favourite area in the kitchen. I like my pantry to be well stocked, with everything in glass jars and sealed containers ready to use when I want to whip up a cake or cook a Thai meal, for example. When an ingredient is finished, I write it straight on my shopping list so I remember to buy it next time I do some food shopping. This way, I never run out of anything.

It is important to keep the pantry clean at all times. Ingredients should be fresh and not past their use-by date.

Group ingredients in your pantry so that they are accessible and complement your lifestyle. For instance, create an area on a shelf specifically for vitamins and supplements to keep them from cluttering your benchtops. You could store them near your breakfast cereals to remind you to take them every morning after you've had your breakfast.

Displaying food items in clean and fashionable containers will change the appearance of your pantry and make it inviting to open the doors. There are many beautiful storage containers and jars available in homeware shops and even supermarkets. These will add a sense of style to your home, so get creative! Put together your own colourful display of ingredients.

Pantry tips

Arrange cans and bottles in rows, with the largest at the back and the smallest at the front. You should be able to see everything in the cupboard when you open the door.

Check use-by dates and discard and replace outdated food.

Buy small, colourful baskets, bowls or containers to use for storing garlic and ginger.

Collect similar-sized glass jars with the same coloured lids, as this will give a uniform theme throughout the pantry.

Ensure that containers are airtight to avoid the ingredients becoming stale or being destroyed by insects.

Group like items together. For example, don't have condiments spread around on lots of shelves. Grouping like items together will save you time choosing the item to use.

Label jars containing food items that are not self-explanatory. For example, 'Self-raising flour', 'Plain flour', 'Corn flour'. Labelling your jars will save you time. If you don't want to stick labels on jars, cut out the label off the packet, including the use-by date, and slip this into the jar so you can see it clearly.

- Place oils in glass bottles or jugs with cork stoppers to give an Italian or French feel.

- Keep potatoes, onions and garlic in a cool, dark place to slow down sprouting and the development of green patches. Store them on an open tray or in a basket as they need to breathe. They will look much more attractive in baskets or trays than in plastic containers or boxes.

- Regularly wipe over shelves in your pantry to keep it clean.

- Recycle spare glass jars. First wash them and remove labels. Use them to store perishable food items like pickles, grated parmesan cheese, olives and sauces for the refrigerator.

 ## Pantry checklist

Following is a list of 'staples' or basic ingredients to have in your pantry to use as a guide. Attach it to the back of your pantry door.

Food type	Ingredient	Need to purchase
Canned food & sauces	Apples, apricots, peaches, plums, mangoes	
	Asparagus	
	Beetroot (sliced/whole)	
	Coconut milk	
	Corn kernels	
	Curry paste	
	Mustard	
	Pasta sauces	
	Peeled tomatoes	
	Tartare sauce	
	Tomato sauce	
Cereals	Breakfast cereals such as bran, corn flakes, lecithin, oats, millet, wheat, and wheat germ.	
	Corn (for popping)	
Dried fruits & nuts	Almonds	
	Apricots	
	Coconut (dried)	
	Pine nuts	
	Raisins	

Food type	Ingredient	Need to purchase
(cont.)	Sultanas	
	Walnuts	
Flours & baking ingredients	Baking powder	
	Baking soda	
	Cocoa powder	
	Corn flour	
	Custard power	
	Icing sugar	
	Plain flour	
	Self-raising flour	
	Sugar	
	Wholemeal flour	
Jams & spreads (*Store spreads for breakfast toast and snacks together on a tray at eye level for easy retrieval*)	Apricot jam	
	Hazelnut spread	
	Peanut butter	
	Marmite	
	Strawberry jam	
	Tahini	
	Vegemite	
Oils & sauces	Vegetable oil (cold pressed)	
	Linseed oil	
	Sesame oil	
	Sunflower oil	

Food type	Ingredient	Need to purchase
Pastas, rice, spaghetti and pulses	Couscous	
	Egg noodles or pasta	
	Fettuccine and spaghetti	
	Lentils (brown and red)	
	Pasta (all sizes)	
	Split peas (yellow)	
	Rice (white or brown)	
Potatoes, garlic and onions	Garlic	
	Onions	
	Potatoes	
Tea and coffee	Coffee	
	Herbal teas	
	Plain tea	
Spices	Allspice (ground)	
	Beef stock	
	Cardamon	
	Chicken stock cubes	
	Chilli (ground)	
	Chilli (fresh)	
	Cinnamon (ground)	
	Coriander (ground)	

Food type	Ingredient	Need to purchase
(cont.)	Cumin	
	Curry powder	
	Garlic flakes	
	Mixed herbs	
	Nutmeg	
	Paprika	
	Peppercorn (black)	
	Saffron	
	Salt (sea salt)	
	Salt (rock salt)	
	Stock cubes	
	Turmeric (ground)	
	Vanilla essence	
	Vanilla pods	

Store large or heavy items such as bags of potatoes, onions, stock of soft drinks, mineral waters and juices, filtered water, cans of oil, wine bottles and cookbooks at the bottom of your pantry. It will be easier to retrieve and replace them if they are stored on lower shelves.

Refrigerator tips

Keep a small bowl of vanilla essence on a shelf at the back of the refrigerator after it has been cleaned to give it a pleasing, fresh smell. (Ensure that it can't be spilt.)

Allow airflow between food to keep the temperature circulating evenly.

Always wrap meat, chicken or fish in plastic wrap and place on a plate to avoid it dripping on other foods. It's best to store raw meats of any kind on the lowest shelf.

Cool hot foods before putting them in the fridge or freezer.

Store dairy products such as butter or margarine, eggs, cheese and yoghurt, as well as condiments and leftover meals, on the top shelf.

Don't eat leftover meals over a day old. Moulds and bacteria develop very quickly and can cause severe intestinal problems.

Clean up any orange juice spills promptly. If orange juice spills on the refrigerator seals, it makes them more prone to splitting.

Wipe up anything that spills in your refrigerator immediately. If you don't, the stickiness will transfer to other items in the refrigerator. Encourage everyone in your house to do this.

- If you are regularly preparing meals in advance and freezing them, write the name of the meal and the date it was prepared on the package before storing it.

- Invest in a good quality frost-free refrigerator so you don't have the hassle of regular manual defrosting.

- Keep ice-block trays filled.

- Keep the door closed after use at all times. It takes time for the refrigerator regulator to readjust to the correct temperature after the door has been opened. Cold air escapes, wasting electricity and costing you money.

- Keep your refrigerator clean. If you can't see the contents at the back of your fridge it's time for a clean out. Do this regularly.

- Use lettuce crispers, as they keep vegetables fresh for longer. Watch out for water accumulating in the bottom of crispers, as this will make vegetables lose their freshness quickly.

- Seal strong-smelling foods such as cheese and fish in airtight containers to prevent odours transferring to other foods.

- Store vegetables in individual bags in the lower drawers of the refrigerator.

8 Your bedroom

Action is eloquence!

William
Shakespeare

Your bedroom is supposed to be a place of rest and relaxation. Avoid having too much clutter in it. The standard items for a bedroom are a comfortable bed that provides good support, a wardrobe or space to hang your clothes, and drawer space for other clothing items such as underwear, socks, jumpers and t-shirts.

You want your bedroom to be free of dust, clean and inviting to be in. It may seem obvious to some people, but changing your sheets regularly can make all the difference to a good night's sleep. Spending time each morning making your bed ensures that you always have a made bed to climb into at the end of the day.

If you are having trouble sleeping, check how much electrical equipment you have in your bedroom. Too much electrical equipment can cause disturbed sleep patterns. If you have an electric clock radio next to the bed along with a television, a video or any other electrical equipment, this can add electrical energy to the room that may hinder your ability to both relax and sleep. Place electrical equipment in purpose-built cabinets away from the bed.

If you don't have storage cabinets or the space for more furniture in your bedroom, cover electrical equipment such as the television or the video player with attractive fabrics to match your bedroom colour scheme to make it look pleasing to the eye. (Ensure that all electrical switches are turned off at the main power while they are covered with fabric.)

If you buy new clothes regularly, periodical clean-outs are a prerequisite to living a clutter-free life. The usual 'rule of thumb' is that if you haven't worn it in a year, get rid of it. This doesn't always apply, depending on how you shop and what you buy. I personally try to buy classic pieces of clothing with colours that don't date so they will last and still look fashionable as much as possible two or three years down the track.

If most things in your wardrobe are out of date and you never wear them, let them go! Fill a bag with clothes to take to a recycled clothing shop or a charity bin. Once you do this, you will be able to see what you really are using. You will also have some space for something new.

Try to allow for roomy hanging space. In this way you will avoid crushing your clothes and having to iron or re-iron them. Always have extra coathangers in the wardrobe so you can hang new clothes immediately. When I buy new items of clothing I try to cull an equivalent number. This creates space for the item. If you don't have any more space in your wardrobe to add new items, it's time to cull or buy a bigger wardrobe. But before you consider this option, ask yourself how many clothes you really need!

Allocate specific places or 'homes' for all the smaller items in your wardrobe. Underwear, socks, belts, ties, beach gear and sports clothes all need a place to 'live', so allocate drawers or other storage holders for these items. Socks can live in colourful baskets; the baskets can have a dual purpose by decorating your room as well as providing storage. You can buy storage systems for all the items in your wardrobe, including ties, belts and shoes.

Tidy up your bedroom daily. Place soiled clothes in a laundry basket each day and keep the dressing table and storage cabinets free of dust.

Make the most of the space usually wasted under your bed. You can purchase narrow plastic storage containers that will slide easily underneath and keep everything dust-free and mould-free. 'Space bags' can also be purchased at storage shops and are useful for storing doonas, blankets and winter clothes during the summer months. If you push all the leftover air out of the bag you will reduce the amount of storage space you need.

When storing memorabilia, choose an extra-special box. It can be a colour you particularly love, or it could be made of wicker, leather or rattan. Ensure that the box has a lid to keep the dust off. Baskets made of materials such as wicker or rattan should be lined with a material of your choice — for example, satin, velvet or plastic — to protect the contents from dust and insects. They should be stored inside your home. You can even put a lock on your basket or box to keep other people or children from looking at your memorabilia without invitation.

Handbags and briefcases

So many people have asked me to show them inside my handbag once they've found out what I do for a living. I think it's really funny and I'm happy to show them. However, for some people keeping handbags or briefcases organised and clutter-free is difficult.

My handbag organises me, so I'm lucky to have found it. It's one of those zippered, compartmentalised, ergonomically designed little black bags that can hold enormous amounts of stuff — if and when it is needed. But I regularly clean it out and get rid of things that don't belong in there. Currently I use this bag for daily use.

My 'daily use' bag has a section allocated for my licence and for business cards, banking cards, health cards etc., and there is another area for personal use where I keep handcream, tissues and make-up. I put my car and home keys in the same spot every time I put them in my bag. I also have a brightly coloured key ring to help me to zoom in on my keys immediately, even if it is dark.

When I go out at night I use a different handbag — one that matches my outfit. I only put in it the basic essentials — keys, lipstick, eyeliner, tissues, drivers licence and of course a credit card or money. That's all you need. Who wants to carry around a big bag with everything in it, including last month's opera program? Keep it simple!

Regular clean-outs

Clean out your bag or briefcase once a week if you can't keep on top of it more regularly than that. Choose Sunday nights to sort it out and get it ready for the week ahead. You only need specific things in your handbag or briefcase, so limit it to that and don't add other items — unless you intend to take them out as soon as you arrive home and have finished for the day.

Tips on maintaining handbags and briefcases

If you plan to be away from the home all day, carry a small supply of 'emergency' needs such as lip cream and tissues, even a toothbrush and toothpaste. (You can buy miniature sizes for handbags, and airlines supply packs of toiletries such as toothpaste, toothbrush, soap and hand creams, which are perfect for handbags or briefcases.)

Your briefcase will reveal to your work colleagues and contacts whether you are organised. Generally, all you need in your briefcase are some business cards; current work-in-progress file or files; notepaper; black, blue and red pens; a pencil; a calculator; Post-It notes; and a good book or magazine to read when needed.

Create a list of the contents of your wallet (in case you lose it). This will make it easier for you to replace everything quickly. List details of all the account numbers of your bank accounts, credit cards (including passwords or pin numbers), medical cards, drivers licence, library and subscription memberships and anything else you usually keep in your wallet. Include details of business cards you use regularly and emergency hotline numbers you need to contact banks and credit card providers in order to 'freeze' cards immediately if your wallet is lost or stolen. Store this list on your computer or in a record book and update it each time a card or piece of information is superseded. (Remember security issues when recording pin numbers on

The bedroom

'Our bedroom and wardrobe need organising as they're out of control and I don't know where to start! Also, we seem to accumulate piles of clutter in our bedroom area.'— Caroline, late forties, married mother of two, works part-time, has a large home, travels and socialises frequently.

Caroline and her husband have a large room off their bedroom for storing clothes and accessories. The room has adequate hanging and shelving space but it needs culling and reorganising to display everything neatly. Piles of clutter have accumulated around the bedroom, including on the bedside tables and on chests of drawers, and piles of paper sit around the perimeter of the room.

A four-hour session is allocated for this process. We start by having four garbage bags on hand to separate items that Caroline doesn't want to keep. The first one is for the charity bin, the second for Caroline's daughter or friends to look at before the items are discarded, the third for items needing repair and the fourth for paper to be recycled. We also have a spare box for items that will 'live' somewhere else in the home.

We start with the hanging spaces. We place items of clothing that Caroline still wears neatly back on coathangers. Once we have sorted the hanging section, we then arrange everything in colour-coordinated sections and hang together items such as matching suit jackets, skirts and trousers. The garbage bags are filling up and more space is being created.

In very little time we complete the hanging section, so we take every-thing off the shelves and out of the drawers to sort and arrange into groups. We discuss the shelf and drawer space usage and I recommend that Caroline place more frequently worn items on the lower shelves. We allocate areas for each category of garment, which makes retrieval and putting away after laundering easier. We wipe clean empty shelves and drawers and leave them to air before replacing anything. We sort through the shelves, placing short-sleeved tops, t-shirts, shorts, scarves, shawls and wraps, thick winter jumpers, thinner wool and cotton jumpers, long-sleeved tops and hats into their groups, then fold or display them neatly. Then we sort through the drawers, placing underwear, stockings, socks, belts, ties, swimming costumes and costume jewellery in their allocated spaces, discarding many items.

When the wardrobe area is complete, we move to the bedroom itself and begin to sift through piles of papers, magazines, books, correspondence and memorabilia. We group items into categories and discard lots of paper and old reading material. Many items on chest tops and bedside tables belong in other areas of the home, so these are put aside to be taken to their appropriate place afterwards. Within four hours the bedroom has been reclaimed and a restful night's sleep is assured. Caroline comments, 'It can be quite draining looking at all this clutter every day and I just didn't have the time or knowhow to resolve it once it got this way ... Now I feel so much better.'

paper or on computers. Keep in mind that you don't need to print the document out — just have it there as a record in case of emergency. It is a good idea to secure your computer with password protection if you are recording bank account details and pin numbers.)

- Women may wish to carry a small mirror in their handbag to check make-up and hair.

- Only carry in your handbag the make-up that you are currently using. Throw out old make-up and keep a small selection in your regularly used bag for day or night wear.

- Regularly clean out all notes and bits of paper. Keep receipts for business expenses in one section of your handbag or in a plastic file in your briefcase. Go through them weekly and separate them into categories.

- Add new telephone numbers to your address book or mobile phone list as soon as you know them.

- Write all appointments in your diary, not on bits of paper in your handbag or briefcase.

9 Children's spaces

> To those who believe that anything is possible ...
>
> St Bernard of Clairaux

Bedrooms

Keep children's bedrooms and spaces fun and bright but, most importantly, simple. Create a storage place for everything in your child's bedroom. Cull clothes, toys and possessions regularly — children outgrow their clothes and toys just like adults outgrow clothes and big toys. If the child is over the age of eight it is a good idea to discuss with them the culling or recycling of toys or clothes. At this age children can communicate clearly, make decisions and know what they like or dislike. Give away outgrown clothes to friends, family or the charity bin. There are also children's recycled clothes shops that will take items on consignment.

Create a space that will reflect your child's unique personality and involve your child in the design. Remember that white doesn't date, so if you paint the walls white you will avoid having to repaint regularly. This also makes it easy to purchase bed linen and decorations, which will never clash with the wall colour. Attach attractive posters and favourite pictures to the walls to add colour. Use Blu-Tack to avoid damage to walls.

Help children to become organised by making it easier and less frustrating to put their things away and find them. Label cupboards and drawers for socks, underwear, t-shirts, jumpers etc. so that the children know where clothes should 'live'. Young children will soon learn to recognise these labels, which in turn will help them learn how to spell. Keep shoes in shoe bags hung at your child's eye level on their wardrobe door. Similarly, hang clothes racks at eye level. Organise to have an adjustable track installed on the inside of your children's wardrobes. This will give you the flexibility to adjust the height of the racks as the children grow. Purchase storage containers in a range of sizes. Keep smaller toys in small storage containers to save children tipping over big containers in the hunt for small items. Make sure the containers are attractive so your child will find it rewarding to put things away. Ensure that the containers you use are easily accessible for small children and that lids won't jam small fingers.

Tips for children's activities

Cut out activity ideas from newspapers and magazines when you see them, and store them for use during holiday periods and travel. Set up a file for each one of your children in your filing cabinet. This will give you a place to store information especially for them and keep clutter at bay.

Purchase beds that have storage drawers in the sides of them, or build an elevated bed so that you can utilise the space underneath for hobbies or a homework or study area.

Playrooms

Make the playroom a space for children to have fun and be creative. Set up areas for specific hobbies or interests. Provide a small table and chair in a corner to allow pre-schoolers to sit and paint or draw. Store all supplies (pencils, crayons, paint, paintbrushes and water jars) in colourful canisters or holders. Lay a waterproof tablecloth over the table to min-imise damage. This can be easily wiped down after use.

Polished floors are best in playrooms because they can be easily mopped and vacuumed. In addition, this surface is durable and attractive. Add colourful rugs to warm the room, and also divide it into sections for different play areas. To prevent a rug slipping from under little feet, secure it to the floor by positioning it over non-slip matting, which you can attach underneath.

Have adequate shelving to store books, rock collections, games, PlayStation equipment and dolls.

Use an old trunk or large bin for storing dress-up clothes. Place in the bin outdated clothes, fancy-dress costumes, old scarves, shoes, hats and coats. This will provide an endless source of creativity for children and entertainment for you!

Run string along a wall in the playroom to have a place to hang artwork. Secure each art piece with pegs. This way you will always have a place to hang paintings or drawings and the artworks can be rotated regularly without damaging walls or cluttering your living rooms or kitchen.

Ask your children to put their toys into allocated storage areas when they have finished playing, then they won't come back to an untidy playroom. Children too can become distressed if a room or house is untidy as it is human nature to want order, not confusion. If children learn to tidy up after themselves they won't have to search for a toy or a part of a toy.

If a toy breaks, get it fixed if possible or throw it away. Broken toys take up precious space and can be hazardous, especially to young children.

Training children

Allocating tasks around the home to your children will save you a lot of energy. Some people may think that children shouldn't be bothered with this sort of 'adult' work until they are much older, if at all. You may think that children need to play and just be themselves, but the younger you start showing your children how to organise their lives and their belongings, the better equipped they will be as young adults to handle their day-to-day lives. By starting them while they are young, you are providing your children with life skills. This will reflect in all areas of their lives.

Children need to experience discipline to learn how to become self-disciplined. Allocating tasks for children to help you in the home has a number of benefits:

- It will educate them in how to look after themselves, which will give them a sense of responsibility.
- It will nurture confidence in them.
- It will encourage them to learn organisational skills from an early age, which will help develop their self-discipline.

The key is for you to be a role model for them as they begin to take responsibility for their bedrooms and play areas. Make it fun. You don't want it to sound like a chore to them; if you do they are likely to mumble, groan or ignore you rather than happily help you out.

Start early, as soon as your children can understand you and can walk. Tell them what you are doing as you put away their toys and play things. Then slowly introduce them to the task in a fun way. Ensure that you have a place for everything so they can learn which box to put their teddies in or which box their games and puzzles live in.

Children love guidelines and routines. In fact, we all do. The optimum ages to train your children, and the activities they can perform, are as follows:

Ages four to eight

Children should easily be able to tidy their own bedrooms as well as tidy up after themselves when they've finished playing in their bedroom or playroom. They should be able to make their own bed, empty small waste bins around the home and deposit their dirty clothes in the laundry basket.

Ages eight to twelve

This age group should be able to lay the table, wash up, put things away, dust, and hang out washing. (You can erect an extra line below the normal clothesline to assist children to hang their own washing and smaller items.)

Teenagers

Teenagers should be able to tackle most household chores. Show them how to take pride in their belongings, keeping their clothes in good order by hanging them neatly in their cupboards, or storing all their belongings in allocated spaces when not in use. Encourage them to put things away where they found them when they have finished using them, as it is tedious having to 'nag' teenagers to tidy their rooms. Teach them how to have discipline by following simple steps each day to add routine to their lives. Then their lives will 'flow' and be easier to deal with.

A task roster

Establish a task roster to share the workload in your family. The roster following can be adapted to your particular circumstances. In addition, ask your children to tidy their rooms for ten minutes before they go to bed each night so they don't wake up to a messy room, which is not a good way to start the day. This also helps children to see how a routine can work efficiently.

* Ask the adult or child with this task to wipe the table down when you have all finished eating and then lay the table for the next meal (provided you don't need to use it in the meantime).

Day	Adult 1	Adult 2	Child 1	Child 2
Monday	Wash up after meals or stack/unstack dishwasher	Free day	Feed the pets	Lay the table for all meals*
Tuesday	Lay the table for all meals*	Collect waste for recycling	Wash up after meals or stack/unstack dishwasher	Feed the pets
Wednesday	Free day	Lay the table for all meals*	Feed the pets	Wash up after meals or stack/unstack the dishwasher
Thursday	Weekly shopping	Wash up after meals or stack/unstack dishwasher	Help with weekly shopping and feed the pets	Lay the table for all meals*
Friday	Lay the table for all meals*	Empty the waste bins	Wash up after meals or stack/unstack the dishwasher	Feed the pets
Saturday	Wash up after meals or stack/unstack the dishwasher	Change towel and bedding	Hang out washing and feed the pets	Lay the table for all meals*
Sunday	Empty the kitchen bin and wash it out	Feed the pets	Lay the table for all meals*	Wash up after meals or stack/unstack the dishwasher

10 The infamous spare room

The spare room generally has a number of purposes. It can act as a guest-room, a home office, a playroom or a 'junk' room. With careful planning you can utilise this space very cleverly to house everything you require (except the 'junk').

If your spare room is full of clutter, de-clutter it (refer to chapter 5), reallocating items to appropriate areas of the house or garage. Sports equipment can be stored in the garage. If you don't have a garage, store equipment on a shelf above the wardrobe area or in the top of a cupboard. If you play a sport like tennis regularly, keep your racquet in an accessible space in the wardrobe.

The guest-room

Get things off the floor and tidy the room so it is ready for the next time a guest arrives. Make sure the sheets are fresh. Cover the bed with a beautiful quilt or a cover made from an attractive fabric. If you have people staying with you regularly, organise the room like hotels do. Place a lamp beside the bed, some good reading material, tissues, a fresh towel and face-washer. In preparation for a guest, add a vase of freshly cut flowers. These small things provide a welcome sign for any visitor. If you invite your guest to treat the room like a home away from home they will surely feel welcome.

You can use spare room cupboards to hold coats and jackets to save space in the wardrobes in *your* bedroom, but try to leave some space for guests to hang their clothes, and have a supply of spare coathangers available for their use.

Open windows and doors to air the room before your guest arrives. A stale-smelling room can cause a bad night's sleep.

The office

Social changes are often reflected in employment practices and these days the number of people working from home is rising dramatically every year. Working from home can give you more time and flexibility, provided you are organised.

Some employers are taking a more flexible approach

towards working conditions, and indeed some encourage their employees to work from home. Many people are self-employed and have structured their businesses in such a way that they can save themselves valuable time and money by working from a home office. There are also many people who are pursuing life-long interests or passions from home in the hope that these will lead to meaningful employment opportunities in the future. Whatever the reason, many of us need a workspace. In many homes today it is as much needed as a kitchen or a bathroom.

Even if you don't run a business from your home, most people need a work area to make telephone calls or pay household accounts. This can be as simple as assigning a special table for the purpose and tucking it away in the corner of a spare bedroom.

If you work at home, you will most likely use the spare room as your home office. Give your office the same attention you give your best client or biggest project. It is where you run your business and personal affairs, and what occurs in this room leads directly to your success in the world.

Being organised in your home office is critical to being productive and powerful. Negative energy is created if there are piles of paper everywhere, files out of place and office equipment lying around. If you have order in your office you will spend less time looking for important papers and therefore will be more productive, so clear out the clutter. It is vitally important to keep routines happening here.

Create a place that you want to go to each day, because if you run your business from home you may be spending between eight and twelve hours there every day. Have the things you love around you and it will be a pleasure to be there. Photos of friends and family, a colourful vase with freshly cut flowers, positive pictures and words of wisdom help to support you in your quest for success. (See further comprehensive information in Part 3: Organising your office.)

If there is simply nowhere in your home or apartment to allocate for your home office needs, you may wish to use screens to divide a room. You can successfully house your home office or workstation behind a screen in a dining room, for instance, using a screen that blends with your decor. Screens are versatile and there are many different materials and designs available. Homeware and import shops usually have an interesting selection. These could solve your space problem.

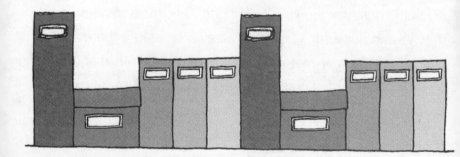

Desk drawers

Keep your desk drawers clutter-free. This saves you wasting time sifting through the clutter piles when looking for something. Some people use their desk drawers for storing their stationery items, others use them for storing current project files and photos. It is a matter of personal preference. I suggest that the top drawer is more often an efficient place to store regularly used stationery items that you need frequently such as pens, stapler, staples, sticky tape, scissors, eraser, ruler, liquid paper, marker pens and paper clips.

If you have a number of desk drawers, allocate specific functions to each drawer then keep it like that. For example, you can have an equipment drawer which could hold your calculator, dictaphone, mobile phone and electronic hand-held diary accessories; a banking drawer to hold current cheque and deposit books; a postage drawer for stamps, your postcode book and business address labels; and a stationery drawer for frequently used items. This way your whole family or staff members will know where to find things when they need to use them.

Notice boards

Don't clutter noticeboards. Regularly remove information that is no longer relevant. Only place pertinent information on

Home office filing system and diary organising

'I need a home for all my paperwork, and I want to be able to use my diary efficiently.'— Jan, fifty-something, a counsellor with three children in their twenties still at home.

Jan has recently re-entered the workforce. She is keen to take better control of her life so she can maintain a busy social and family life.

Jan's home office has purpose-built file drawers in a fitted desk unit built along a wall. There is also a great deal of storage space for books and magazines above it. She has a basic filing system in place already but it needs to be reviewed and made more functional. In addition, Jan's desk is piled high with papers and 'things to do'.

The first thing Jan needs to do is to sort all the paperwork into categories, then reorganise the filing system, creating a hanging file for each new file category and providing a place for everything. One drawer will be allocated to business matters and the other to personal and family issues. Magazine boxes can be purchased so that different magazine subscriptions can be placed in separate boxes, ordered by month and date. These will be stored on top of the built-in filing drawers, giving Jan a ready-made place to put everything off her desk.

Jan has accumulated quite a collection of diaries and Filofax inserts and has been trialling different diaries to see which one works best for her. It seems that the accumulation of so many styles has added to Jan's confusion. Besides trying to use a diary, Jan keeps a month calendar on her desk, which allows her to see her commitments for a whole month at a glance.

The month calendar system works well for Jan, but she needs to transfer the information into the diary she carries with her every day. Although Jan prefers to maintain a paper diary and calendar system, we do discuss portable electronic personal organisers as an alternative. Jan has recently learned how to use e-mail, and no doubt it is only a matter of time before she will become interested in exploring electronic organisational tools further.

For the moment it is important to identify Jan's needs and select the diary that suits those needs best. After some discussion it emerges that the kind of diary that best meets Jan's needs is one with separate sections for specific purposes. (We have previously listed the various functions that Jan expects of her diary.) Jan decides she needs a section in her diary where she can write ideas for gifts and another for personal reflections. In this way she can always have her ideas with her when she is out shopping. In addition, I suggest she use Post-It notes for recording action items each day and shopping lists. Jan can attach the Post-it notepad to the inside of her diary.

We agree that Jan needs to set aside two to four hours each week to look at her paperwork on a regular basis. Jan blocks this set time in her diary. She intends to use the time to file papers and action-pending items.

After two four-hour sessions per month for twelve months, Jan now has more control over her life. She is more in touch with what is happening with her family, her social life and her work. It suits Jan best to continue to work with me for two sessions per month. One session enables Jan to keep on top of day-to-day paperwork and bill payments, and the other allows her time for planning and actioning new projects.

your noticeboard. Information on your noticeboard should be for immediate use and it should be relatively small and neatly placed. Noticeboards can also hold memorabilia such as photos of friends or family, beautiful cards you have received, information that relates to your business or project, and interesting business cards.

Another noticeboard could be hung specifically to pin up media exposure you have received or letters that you have sent out but have not received a response to. (Pin papers at the top left corner so they hang down below the board to save space.) Bulldog clips can also be hung from pinboard pins to hold heavier information.

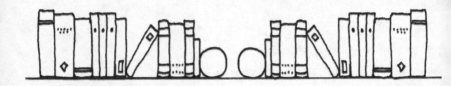

11 Personal finances

> *Begin difficult things while they are easy. Do great things when they are small. The difficult things of the world must once have been easy; the great things must once have been small … A thousand mile journey begins with one step.*
>
> Lao Tse

'I never know where to put my bills and they seem to end up on the bottom of the pile of papers that accumulate — and so I forget them, until a reminder comes in the mail.' This is a common scenario. The way to organise bills is to create one place for them. This may be a hanging file in your filing cabinet or a display folder specifically designed for holding outstanding bills. Your bills should never get out of hand if you have a place to put them. Practise the routine of checking them at a set time each week.

Organising personal finances is a key area of everyone's life, but so often it is the last area to be looked at. Your finances require constant attention and regular maintenance to stay abreast of change. For example, interest rates rise and fall, affecting your mortgage payments or interest; bank fees change; and new ways of paying bills become available. By implementing simple routines and learning how to access new options available to us, we can speed up the processes that must be done to keep the money in our lives flowing.

How to organise a bill payment folder

Purchase a display folder with at least twenty clear plastic pages inside. When a bill comes in the mail, highlight the amount due and the due date with a highlighter pen. This allows you to see details clearly at a glance, without having to search through the bill for this information.

Place the bill in the folder, ordered by due date. The bill that needs to be paid first should be at the front of the folder. With all your bills arranged in this way you can see at a glance the companies you owe money to and when they have to be paid. Choose a day of the week to check the folder to ensure that bills are paid on time.

Use your bill payment folder to hold application forms or purchase order forms you need to fill in. For example, you may wish to subscribe to a new magazine or buy a book or gift.

Are your finances disorganised?

If you are disorganised in any way financially you need to reassess everything step by step. Have a look at the way you are handling your money and what you owe, and set in place a budget with strict guidelines for future spending. A financial planner will be able to help you to assess your goals and to set yourself up for a brighter future. There is a way out of financial disorganisation æ you just need to ask for assistance and be dedicated to changing your situation at all costs (pardon the pun).

A book called *The Courage To Be Rich* by Suze Orman is worth reading if you are interested in changing your mental attitude to the way you view money. The book suggests that it is possible to shift your thinking and that with a new attitude to money you can create the kind of lifestyle you really want. Orman outlines a number of processes and skilful steps that can help you achieve the goals you set yourself. According to Orman, following these steps will bring a more abundant and satisfying life.

Getting organised with Internet banking

The home computer is making it easier for us to use many services from the comfort of our home, so take full advantage of it. Internet banking is the way of the future so it's time to start learning how to use it. No-one wants to spend time in bank queues today. We don't have the time or the personal energy to waste anymore.

Once you learn how to log into your bank's website you will have access to your records twenty-four hours a day, seven days a week. You will be able to:

- change your access code and password
- check account balances
- check fixed-term investments
- check your loan details
- display periodical payment details
- enquire about a loan
- find out how much interest you've earned
- pay your bills
- request forms (or download forms without having to wait for them by mail)
- review transaction details
- transfer funds
- update your address or phone details
- view your latest statement.

Telephone banking

A useful option for paying your bills is to use 'BPay' or telephone banking using your bank's telephone banking service. This saves loads of time and the inconvenience of having to leave your home. Older people and people with disabilities in particular can save themselves effort and energy when paying bills and transferring funds by doing this over the telephone.

12 Living rooms and family rooms

Consider the purpose of your living room. Is it a place to relax and unwind? A place to spend quality time with your family and friends? A place to read and listen to music? To watch television or videos? Or is it a formal entertaining area?

For many, the living room is the most used and visible area of the home, although activities vary depending on the occupants of the household. We may display our collections of knick-knacks and books or precious artworks or we may carry out tasks like household paperwork, ironing, homework projects and hobbies. In addition, activities like watching television and listening to music create the need for a space that is flexible and adequately organised.

Essential items of furniture include comfortable seating,

side tables on which people may place drinks, a decent-sized coffee table, and a place to store books and magazines. If you like displaying ornaments, ensure there is a designated space for them. When organising this room, think about what it is used for and plan it accordingly. Go through old books and take the ones to be thrown out to a secondhand bookshop or opportunity shop. You don't want your shelves to be cluttered. Have a handyman build extra shelves if you need more storage or more space to add new books to your library.

Tips for living rooms and family rooms

Avoid over-burdening double adaptors. Instead, purchase powerboards to extend your outlet capability. Electricians and fire authorities advocate this as a much better option than using double adaptors.

Add bookshelves to unused wall space to increase storage capacity.

Cull magazines regularly and put them into the recycling bin or offer them to your local doctor's waiting room. Alternatively, offer them to a kindergarten where they can be used to cut out pictures.

Discard old newspapers once they have been read.

- In the past, electrical outlets restricted the placement of furniture and equipment, but today extension cables can be used. Position them around the perimeter of the room, enabling you to move furniture to just the right place in the room.

- Keep the television guide in a set place. When the new one arrives, throw the old one out straight away.

- Mount televisions and other electrical equipment on walls to save floor space.

- Store remote controls for the television, video, stereo or DVD in one drawer or storage basket for easy retrieval.

- Build in a window seat. They are great for storage.

Regular tidy-ups

Keeping your home tidy each day is just a matter of straightening things out. Put on some loud, groovy music to uplift and inspire you while you work! Tidying and cleaning *can* be fun! Open the windows and doors to air the rooms as you tidy. Follow these simple routines:

- Bathroom: Ensure that towels are hung neatly on towel rails, wipe down wet basins and bench surfaces and generally restore order to the room. Make sure you have adequate space for each towel to hang to ensure that the room looks tidy and that the towels dry after each use. (You may wish to install a heated towel rail.)

- Bedrooms: Fold back bedding to allow it to air and perspiration to dry. Make the bed later.

- Dining room: Clear dining table surfaces and wipe over. Arrange all items neatly on the sideboard.

- Kitchen: Wash up after each meal. Tidy and wipe all bench surfaces.

- Living rooms: Place magazines and newspapers in a neat pile. Put remote controls in their designated drawer or storage box. Puff cushions and arrange them neatly on lounges.

- Pets: Clean pet food dishes.

The living room

'I have loads of paperwork that needs sorting, and no space in my home to store anything. I'd love to reclaim my lounge room.' — Rebecca, single, works full-time quite a distance from her home and loves creative hobbies in her spare time.

Rebecca lives in a three-bedroom house. She has accumulated masses of paper, craft materials and general household items in her living spaces because she hasn't had the time to maintain them. There are three four-drawer filing cabinets in two spare bedrooms, but they are filled to the brim. One room is dedicated to craft materials and hobby books and there is no space to add anything else. Rebecca hasn't been able to identify specific places to store her items, and is reluctant to throw anything away for fear she may need it 'one day'.

On our first meeting, progress sorting through everything is slow and time-consuming because Rebecca doesn't want to throw anything away. I assure her that the outdated newsletters, magazines, advertising and correspondence (some dating back ten years) from many different organisations — such as banks, credit unions and associations she has belonged to — will not be missed if discarded. She only needs to keep the most recent information (the last year). We manage to fill a large garbage bag with paper to be recycled.

Rebecca agrees to establish an archive system for old but important records such as bank statements, tax receipts and records, investment statements and performance information, personal memorabilia and photos. This will create space for current information. Once the filing cabinet drawers are ready, we move information from the floors and other surfaces to the file drawers. We list the contents of each archive box. We clear space on her living room floor, on her desk and in the desk drawers. She now has a 'place for everything'.

This first session is very much a 'letting go' experience for Rebecca, who has become trapped by her habit of surrounding herself with 'stuff' that she does not seem to notice. (From my experience the subconscious does notice mess, but many people choose not to look at it. However, simply knowing that something should be done about the problem becomes a stress.)

My second session with Rebecca is much easier for her and she is more enthusiastic when discarding items. She is excited about the changes that have occurred. She can see spaces on the floor and feels more in control.

For the third session, Rebecca asks me to go to her home while she is at work. She is now able to trust me to discard and organise without her overseeing the process. She informs me that her family has been helping her with other rooms, and when I arrive her bedroom has been cleared and organised. By the time the third visit is complete, most items in her living room have been sorted and she is now able to invite friends and family over to socialise. Rebecca has made a huge leap. By changing her habits she has created order in her home, making way for a better life and a future she can look forward to.

Useful things to keep on hand in your home

- book of postage stamps
- broom
- candles
- dust-pan and broom
- elastic bands
- emergency toolkit
- envelopes (including airmail envelopes)
- extension cord
- first-aid kit
- greeting cards for all occasions
- matches
- notepaper: A4 and small writing paper
- paper towel roll
- pen or pencil
- plastic bags in different sizes with airtight seals
- small spade
- spare batteries for all equipment in the house
- spare electrical double adaptor
- spare light globes
- spare pair of rubber gloves
- string
- tea-light candles
- tissues
- toilet paper
- torch (with live batteries)

13 Treasured memories and important dates

> *Work is love made visible.*
>
> Kahlil Gibran

Photographs

Photograph storage seems to be a problem for many people and it's generally a task that gets left till last. We say, 'one day I'll get around to my photos' or 'next holiday, I'm going to get all my photos in order' æ but the time comes and guess what? We've got better things to do!

We are forever taking snaps of our travels, our children's lives, every moment that seems important in our life. We keep photos of occasions to keep as memories so we can have a record of our lives. We want to be able to look at them when we like, to remind us of that special person or time we had.

Very often photos are just tossed into a big box, or strewn throughout cupboards all over the house, in no order. The job seems daunting to say the least, and a lot of hard work is needed to get them into a system so we can view them easily.

The good news is that there are solutions — it doesn't *need* to be a huge job. Today we have a few different storage options available to us to make the task easier.

Photograph albums

There is a wide range of photo albums of different types, sizes and colours to choose from. For example, if you want to keep photos for a particular occasion in one album, you can purchase albums especially for the number of prints you have. These albums can store anything from 25 to 500 regular-sized prints.

You can find albums in many colours and in many stylish materials. You can have a photograph album specially made to the size you like, with the flexibility to be able to add pages when necessary.

Some people keep photo albums in a series, starting their collection from birth, with special occasions recorded throughout their life following on from each other. You may wish to create separate albums for special occasions such as weddings, christenings and birthday parties.

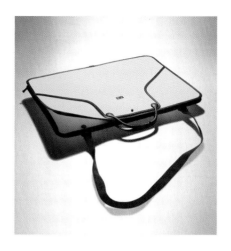

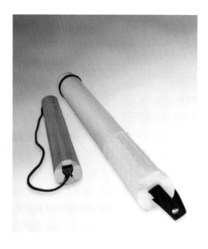

From top left, clockwise: M.H. Way Arabica case, Zoom, Partner folders, Secretaire and Luce bag.

From top: Papaya baskets and archive boxes; assorted boxes and folders from Trusty Boxes & Cases.

From top: Trusty Boxes & Cases storage box and photo archive box.

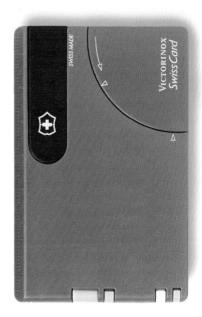
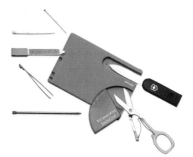
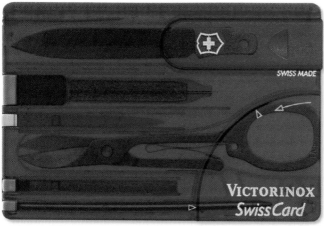

From top left, clockwise: The Booksling from US Huus; the SwissCard from Victorinox.

Photograph storage boxes

Photograph storage boxes come in colourful designs and can
be purchased at most photographic stores. They are designed
to hold many different packs of photos. You will find this to be
the easiest way to keep in order the photos you have not put
in albums. In addition, storing your photos in this way will
keep them dust-free and clean.

The boxes come with hard cardboard dividers to divide
your packs of photos. The dividers have 'title' tabs at the top,
so when you take the lid off the box it looks like a small filing
cabinet. The labels could read 'New Year's Eve 2001 – Calypso
party', 'Barb & Rob's new baby', 'Mum and Dad's 50th wedding
anniversary lunch', 'Company Christmas party', etc. List on the
card at the front of the box the occasions and dates so you
can see at a glance what photos you have in the box. You can
stack these boxes on shelves in colourful collections or in a
corner of the room. Choose different coloured boxes for
different parts of your life — for example, blue for work and
purple for personal.

How to sort out photographs and store them in photograph storage boxes

1   Take all the packs of photographs you have and sit them on a table.

2   Take out of the first pack the best photos only. Cull out the shots that are overexposed, underexposed or blurred, or that don't appeal.

3   Finish this process with all of the packs you have.

4   The process may take some time unless you can look at them objectively and quickly make a decision about the quality of the print. Later when you have them in boxes or albums, you can gaze at them till your heart's content. If you have children, try to choose a time when they are asleep or at a friend's place, otherwise they are bound to want to look at all the photos with you.

5   You may have loose photos from prints given to you. Just keep the best and make a pile of the rest. (The rest are the ones to be thrown away.)

6   Now that the culling is done, take your first pack and put the photos in chronological order by date. Then move onto the next.

7   Once you have finished this process, take your first pack and write the occasion name on the 'title' tab. Then put the pack of photos in the box behind the tab.

8   Work through all the packs like this, stacking them behind one another.

You now have a perfectly organised, neat, colourful, stylish selection of photo boxes to look through whenever you choose. (Set aside half a day to begin with to do, say, 20 packs.)

If you are reluctant to throw away any photos, remember that you will always have the negatives to reprint from if you need to one day. Store the negatives behind the photos in the box or clipped to the 'title' tab.

Anniversaries

How often have you said, 'Oh no! I've forgotten my brother's birthday — how did that happen?' or forgotten an important anniversary. You then end up sending a 'belated' card, which serves as a reminder to the recipient that you forgot. Here are some handy tips to help you remember all the dates that are important to you without ever having to worry again.

Anniversary checklist

▓ Write or type up a list of all the anniversaries you need to remember so you will always have a record.

▓ Write the names of all the important people in your life on your list. Include family, friends and work associates.

▓ For everyone on your list, find out birthdays or other important anniversary dates. Enter this information onto your list.

▓ Go through your diary and write all birthday or anniversary information on the relevant day in red.

▓ When you open your diary to a particular week or when planning ahead, you will always see the entries in red. This way you can plan ahead to send a card or buy a gift when appropriate.

Another approach is to purchase 'personal organiser' software for your computer or use a hand-held diary (better known as a PalmPilot). Enter all the dates you wish to remember, then reminders will happen automatically. You will never need to remember these dates again.

Wedding anniversaries — what to give

Traditionally, gifts made of a particular substance were given to celebrate wedding anniversaries. For those of you who enjoy tradition, here is a list of what to give on each wedding anniversary.

Year	Gift	Year	Gift
First	Cotton	Thirteenth	Lace
Second	Paper	Fourteenth	Ivory
Third	Leather	Fifteenth	Crystal
Fourth	Silk or flowers	Twentieth	China
Fifth	Wood	Twenty-fifth	Silver
Sixth	Sugar or iron	Thirtieth	Pearl
Seventh	Wood or copper	Fortieth	Ruby
Eighth	Bronze	Forty-fifth	Coral
Ninth	Pottery	Fiftieth	Gold
Tenth	Tin	Fifty-fifth	Emerald
Eleventh	Steel	Sixtieth	Diamond
Twelfth	Silk, fine linen or leather	Seventieth	Platinum

14 Recycling

> *In the end, these things matter most;*
> *How well did you love? How fully did you live? How well did you learn to let go?*
>
> Anon

Recycling has been topical for the past ten years and is, out of necessity, the way of the future. You can recycle just about anything these days. Many people are open to the idea of buying something secondhand. What was once someone's trash will become another's treasure, and you can find many people on weekends out hunting around for a secondhand bargain at garage sales, recycled fashion shops or factory seconds shops. You never know what you may find, which is part of the excitement of shopping this way.

All state governments in Australia have developed resources to assist with recycling and some advertise on television and in magazines to ensure we are kept aware of the need to reduce waste. Most local councils have programs in place to take away our recycled materials at specified times of the week, month and year, which is helping enormously to de-clutter our homes and backyards. Take advantage of the service available and put your paper, plastic, glass and garden refuse out when your local council comes to collect. (I'd rather do this than take a trip to the tip!)

State and territory government websites are a good resource. In particular, the New South Wales Government has a directory on its website that tells you where you can buy recycled products such as building materials, furniture, office furniture, garden and outdoor equipment, household items, packaging, animal care products and automobile products, to name a few. (See appendix A for state government and territory Websites and organisations concerned with recycling and disposal. Telephone numbers are listed in the *White Pages* telephone directory under the Government section or your local council.)

What to do with old books and magazines

We often become attached to the books that have given us insights and enjoyment, so culling them can be an emotional task. Once we have read them, however, many books are never looked at again unless they are a source of reference for work

or interests. At some time we may have to clear space on our bookshelves for new books that we purchase or are given as gifts.

After sorting through them and selecting those you wish to dispose of, do one or more of the following:

- Give them away to friends or family.
- Offer them to your local library or a retirement village or nursing home.
- Sell them at a secondhand bookstore.
- Hold a garage sale.
- Get together with a group of friends and organise a market stall to sell your books, along with other 'junk' that you don't want any more. You will make some money and have some fun.

Offer magazines that are in good condition to your hairdressing salon, your local doctor or dental surgery for their waiting rooms, or a hospital. You can also give magazines to the local kindergarten for children to cut out pictures.

15 Bathrooms

Grooming and hygiene are the primary uses of this room, so remove anything that doesn't relate to these processes immediately. The bathroom is a place to recharge, refresh and prepare yourself for the world, and you only need certain things in it to help you do this. Keep it clean and uncluttered and this will provide some calm and tranquillity in your life.

Install adequate towel rails to hang all towels. Stand-alone towel racks can provide extra space. Most items needed in a bathroom are reasonably small, so storage should not be a problem. Utilise available wall space to hang extra cabinets or shelves. Wicker storage baskets can be used to store spare towels. Roll up towels to display them, rather than stacking

them. This will save space. If you have the space, move in a wardrobe or add some shelves for further storage.

Medical supplies can be stored on plastic trays in a separate area of your cabinet or, if there are small children in your home, up high in a lockable cabinet. Check expiry dates on medicines and drugs and throw away outdated drugs regularly. Women should go through make-up and regularly throw away items more than a year old. Even the most expensive brands expire quickly.

Keep on hand a stock of regularly used items such as toilet paper, toothpaste, soaps, shampoo and conditioner, moisturiser, cotton balls, cotton buds and tissues. When you see that you have used the last of an item, or are about to do so, add it on your shopping list to remind you to buy some more.

Create a space that is a haven for relaxation when you need it — a place to relax and unwind, to cleanse the body and soul. It's nice to have an oil burner to burn some relaxing oils during bath-time. It may calm the kids as well! (Remember that oils should be diluted, just a few drops added to water, and never leave your burner unattended.)

Essential bathroom requirements for all the family

- bucket or storage bin to hold cleaning equipment (for example, all-purpose cleaner, toilet cleaner, rubber gloves, scourer and sponge)
- cleansing masks, cleansers and toners
- comb and brush
- conditioner
- cotton buds
- cotton wool
- dental floss
- deodorant
- disposable nappies
- exfoliaters
- exfoliating mitt
- face-washers
- hairdryer
- hand cream
- hand towels
- make-up, nail varnish and nail varnish remover.
- moisturiser
- sanitary napkins and tampons

- shampoo
- shaving brush
- shaving cream
- shaving razors
- shower cap
- small waste bin (lined with plastic bag for easy disposal of rubbish)
- soap
- storage bin to hold bath-time toys for small children
- talcum powder
- tissues
- toilet brush
- toilet paper (always keep an extra supply on hand)
- tools of the trade: tweezers, nail-clippers, nail-file, small scissors
- toothbrushes
- toothpaste
- towels

16 The laundry

And the day came when the risk to remain tight in a bud became more painful than the risk it took to blossom.

Anon

This room doesn't need to be a constant reminder of chores. If you don't have a separate designated laundry room, keep your washing machine and clothes dryer, along with everything that goes with them, in a purpose-built cupboard or behind a curtain that can be closed between uses.

 Tips for the laundry

☀ Collect all dirty laundry items at one time from throughout your house and sort them into washing loads. You may do this a number of times a week, but in most cases it's not necessary to wash every day.

- Be conscious of the weather and take advantage of fine days. No one wants to have wet clothes lying around the house.

- Use efficient equipment. Good washing machines and dryers are designed to save time æ lots of it.

- Use storage baskets on shelves as the designated areas for dividing washing into three groups: whites, darks and general coloured washing. Ask your family or housemates to sort their clothes into each of these three areas when they need washing. This will save you time sorting. Also, train your children!

- Store laundry detergents and the like on shelves in plastic or woven basket trays. Choose your favourite colours and styles to suit your taste, ensuring that items can sit neatly on them with labels facing out so you can see everything clearly.

- Store cleaning products and equipment for the whole house in the laundry.

Essential laundry and cleaning items

The following is a general list of cleaning and laundering products that will assist you in keeping your home spick and span.

- bleach (powders such as Napi-San work well for whitening anything)
- broom
- bucket(s)
- chamois leather (better known as the 'chammy')
- disinfectant liquid
- dusters
- dusting brush/broom
- dust-pan and brush
- fabric softener
- furniture polish
- general all-purpose cream cleanser or scouring liquid for 'hard-to-do' areas
- laundry detergent (liquid or powder)
- linseed oil (for oiling timber furniture)
- old toothbrush (to clean awkward areas)
- pegs
- rubber gloves (have two pairs as they can tear easily)
- scouring pads
- scrubbing brush
- soap-filled scouring pads
- sponge mop
- sponges
- stain remover
- starch (for ironing)
- vacuum cleaner bags
- washing cloths
- window cleaner
- wool wash

One of my friends says she saves an enormous amount of time by pre-sorting soiled washing. She can grab a load at any time and put it in the washing machine without having to go through the process of sorting it out. In fact, she would like to have eight laundry baskets in a row in her laundry if she had the space, labelled as follows:

- Whites
- Darks
- Men's coloured
- Women's coloured
- Kids' clothes
- Linen
- Towels and sheets
- Hand-washing

All the containers would be identical and stylish, in either basketweave or canvas.

Try it! Train your spouse, partner, flatmate or children to deposit their washing in appropriately labelled baskets.

If you don't have adequate space in your laundry for this many baskets, or don't have the need, set up baskets to separate washing loads into three categories: whites, darks and general colours.

17 Functional garages and sheds

> *If you don't know where you are going, then how will you get there? VISUALISE! Make pictures in your mind. See the destination. Imagine your arrival.*
>
> Bryce Courtenay

Before getting organised here, it is important to decide what the main function of the garage or backyard shed is. It could be used as:

- a place to house a vehicle
- a rainy day playroom for the kids
- a storage area for recreational items
- a work area for pursuing a hobby
- a workstation for repairing household items
- a workshop for maintaining vehicles or other mechanical items
- somewhere to pot seedlings and store garden requirements.

Organising the garage or backyard shed

Before you start, think about which items you wish to retain and where the most practical or accessible position for them will be. Draw a rough plan of the space to decide where you will place things.

1   Take everything out.

2   If it will be too disruptive to do the whole area at once, tackle the space section by section.

3   As items are taken out of the area, organise them into groups, like with like.

4   Throw out as much as possible. For example, if that old airbed you find has a hole in it, ask yourself if you are ever going to fix it. If the answer is 'no', dispose of it. If you are motivated to fix the airbed, think about the opportunities you will create. You can go camping again or go floating down a gently flowing river for an afternoon. (Ideal for that spare time you are creating by being more organised!)

5   Clean the area as you go. Wipe over tools and objects that will be retained in the newly organised space so they look as good as they can. Place them to one side until it's time to put them back in an ordered fashion.

6   Sweep the empty space. If it's practical to do so, you may wish to hose it down. Let it dry before you put things back.

7   Dust and wipe down all benches, walls, doors, windows, etc. Don't forget the cobwebs on the walls and in the rafters. Clean dirty areas with a heavy-duty cleanser such as Ajax.

8   Take a break after all that hard work. Have a cup of tea, a glass of water, a wine or a beer. Put your feet up for fifteen minutes æ you've earned it! Sit, sip and relax. You will feel relief that the most daunting part of the task is over.

9   Don't stop now. After you've rested, get back to it!

10 When you put things back, aim to make the space as user friendly as possible. Group together like items or items used for a similar purpose or task. Remember, the idea is to create one place for each group of items, not five.

Handy tools and equipment

If you organise your tools and equipment into groups, you will find it easier to check whether you have all the necessary items to complete particular types of tasks. Here are some checklists for each key group.

Garden tools checklist

- brushcutter or edge-trimmer
- containers for storing seedlings, potting mix, fertilisers and weed-killers (Make sure that chemicals such as weed-killers are clearly marked and stored on a high shelf, well out of reach of children.)
- fork (large)
- gardening gloves
- garden shears
- lawn mower
- rake
- rubber boots or gardening clogs (these are very useful)
- secateurs
- spade (large)
- trowel (for potting plants).

Shelves can be useful for storing smaller gardening items.

Workshop tools checklist

- *concreting tools such as trowels for different-sized tasks (for fine-finishing corners or paint-scraping)*
- *drill*
- *drill attachments (drill and screwdriving bits, sanding discs, wire brushes, etc.)*
- *hammer*
- *multi-grips*
- *paintbrushes, paint tins, paint rollers*
- *pliers*
- *set of screwdrivers (in a variety of sizes)*
- *socket set*
- *spanners (in a variety of sizes).*

Pre-holed particleboard can be useful for displaying tools on the wall. Arrange tools in order of size. Have everything hanging on your walls to utilise space that may otherwise be wasted.

Toolbox checklist

Most hardware stores sell ready-made (or specially designed) toolbox cases to keep your tools organised. These have different compartments to separate items according to size. Invest in one of these so you will have a place to keep all your tools safely. Useful tools include:

- file
- fuse wire
- hacksaw
- hammer
- nails (a few different sizes)
- paint scraper
- paintbrush (small)
- plane
- pliers
- retractable steel tape measure (at least three metres long)
- screwdrivers (various sizes)
- screws
- spanner
- Stanley knife
- string.

Keeping your tools organised

It can be frustrating when we look for a hammer, for example, to do some home repairs, only to find it's not in its place. Often, as a result, the task will be put on hold, along with all those other unfinished projects, until we find it. How much easier and more efficient it would be if we found our tools where they were supposed to be each time.

Develop the habit of returning your tools to the space allocated when you've finished with them. Next time you walk into the garage or backyard shed you will find that everything will be in its place. You won't have to waste time searching anymore æ that hammer will be just where it is meant to be.

Aim to keep together tools that relate to certain tasks. There are a number of alternative ways these can be stored. For instance, each group of tools could be stored in its own toolbox or storage bin, or assigned to a specific set of shelves.

Decide whether more shelving or a workbench is required. If you need more shelves, buy or build them and mount them.

Maintenance

Keep all tools well maintained. For example, after you use a cutting tool, check the blade. If it is not as sharp as it should be, sharpen it *before* returning it to its place. Then, next time it is required, there will be one less job to be done. Keeping all tools and equipment well maintained will also prolong their life. Tools often become rusty if they're used in the rain or simply from moisture in the air, particularly in coastal areas. To extend the life of your tools, develop the habit of wiping them down after you've used them, and keep them dry.

Equipment such as lawn-mower blades, secateurs and chainsaws will require regular sharpening.

18 Storage

There are many places in which to store your possessions. You can use cupboards; wardrobes; armoires; boxes made of wood, cardboard, plastic or aluminium; woven baskets; containers made of plastic or glass; or shelving. You can use hooks and coathangers. There are functional solutions for storing everything you own.

Plan for adequate storage when assessing your home or business storage needs. If you purchase a house that has little storage you can have purpose-built storage constructed. Get creative. Have shelves built for spaces underneath stairs or in attics — anywhere that is not being used that could be. You can have free-standing shelves built if you live in a space that is rented. This will enable you to take the shelves with you when you leave.

Storage ideas

Trolleys on wheels are a great idea for storing stationery items or artists' tools such as paintbrushes, paints, pencils and pens; or use them to carry items from the kitchen to your garden when you are entertaining. Trolleys can be wheeled into a cupboard or under a desk when not in use.

Converting old shoeboxes into storage containers is an option that will take very little effort. Using recycled or leftover gift wrap and some glue, you can cover boxes in different textured and coloured paper. Alternatively, purchase attractive fabrics to cover boxes with the intention of matching storage containers with your furniture and interior design features.

If you are considering moving to a bigger home because you need more storage space, think before taking this drastic step. Try being more creative with the space you have. Look around and try to identify new storage spaces. You might have overlooked some areas. There may be wall space that is not being utilised in your living area or children's room, a space under a staircase, or a poorly designed pantry or wardrobe that can be reworked. Of course, after you've done this exercise you may still think, 'There's no more spare space, that's why we need to move to a bigger house.'

Steps to identifying and creating more space for storage

1   Go through each room, one by one, and check all four walls to see what space is free.

2   Imagine the shape of the storage unit that could fit in this free space. For instance, you may say, 'I could fit a two-metre tall cupboard in the space near the back door that is currently only used for runners and boots. The space above the floor is wasted.' You may say, 'I could build three rows of stylish bookshelves on either side of the fireplace using that bare wall for our rapidly increasing book library.' There are many solutions today and very often wall space can be found to be under-utilised storage space.

3   Now look at all the storage cabinets you have. Look for unused space, such as above your stored possessions. If there is space here and it is not being used, you could quite easily build in some more shelves. Consult a handyman, cabinet-maker or architect to get ideas. If you prefer not to enlist a professional, see how creative you can be yourself. Most people are capable of fitting their house out with great storage products and furniture ideas since there are so many ready-made resources to choose from.

Space-saving ideas

Here are some space-saving ideas for the various rooms of your home and for the garage.

Kitchens

- Install baskets, divider racks, trays, sliding shelves or turntables to avoid losing items at the back of a deep cupboard or shelving.

- Install wire racks inside the pantry door or inside doors under the sink for easy access to smaller items.

- Store spice bottles in a drawer space rather than on a shelf. Place sloped racks in the drawer to display the spice labels so you can read them easily, and arrange the spices in alphabetical order. This method of storage also keeps bottles dust-free.

- Attach a plastic rubbish bin to the inside of a cupboard door or pantry to utilise this space, or use a bin on wheels to manoeuvre around the kitchen when you are preparing food. It can be stored neatly in a cupboard.

- Collect used food jars in all shapes and sizes, wash them thoroughly, remove old labels and reuse them for storing perishable foods such as grains, nuts, herbs and spices and stewed fruits. You can also find elegant bottles in homeware shops for storing items such as detergent by the sink so you don't have to use up valuable cupboard space. Buy glass rather than plastic so you can recycle the jars. (Label bottles clearly to identify the contents. Sticky labels from the newsagent or stationer are useful.)

Babies' and children's rooms

Use stackable plastic crates on castors to store toys so you can move them from room to room easily. Your children will be able to manoeuvre them too with little effort.

A 'trundle' bed makes the best of sense in children's rooms. A trundle bed is a bed built in under the main bed that can slide in and out as required. It can be pulled out at a moment's notice for a friend to stay.

A Lego mat is the best place for Lego blocks to be stored. Buy or make a quilted mat large enough for a few small children to play on. To store the blocks when not in use, take each corner of the mat and join them together, then tie a colourful ribbon around the top and put it away in a cupboard. Remember to store the ribbon safely in a drawer or out of little children's hands when it's not in use. (Courtesy of Louise Scott)

Living rooms

Use a coffee table with a shelf or drawer at the side or underneath for storing pens, magazines and the television and sound system remote controls.

When there is limited floor space for a television set, attach a bracket to the wall, placed at the ideal height and angle, and hang your television from it. (Note: Consider the positioning of the television very carefully before mounting it. Putting up the mountings for this purpose is a major job, so positioning the television incorrectly will enlarge the process. When mounting a television on a wall, ensure that it is accessible to everyone in the room and positioned ergonomically to avoid neck strain.)

Store your television, sound system and video in a cabinet or storage unit so they are out of sight when not in use. This will give an uncluttered feeling to your living room. The more things you can store out of sight, the more you will feel a sense of order and calm.

Bathrooms

Small bathrooms often require extra storage facilities. Use stackable baskets, under-sink trolleys, pegs, hooks and shelves to give you more space for those smaller storage requirements.

Laundries

A spare portable clothes rack on wheels is a bonus in wet weather to hang clothes to dry. I find it invaluable when it looks like rain and the clothes on the line are nearly dry. Whip them off and hang shirts, dresses and tops on coathangers on this rack and they will dry overnight. When it's not in use, fold it up and store it in a cupboard.

Garages

Storage in garages can be increased by installing high shelves or racks to store surfboards, bicycles, camping equipment, sporting equipment or paint. Suspend panels from or fix them across ceiling beams to store unused timber lengths and fishing rods.

Allocate a large trunk or plastic storage bin for all your camping needs: plates, mugs and cups, cutlery, napkins, cooking utensils and small plastic storage containers for leftover food and pre-pared meals. A similar-sized bin can be used to store sleeping bags, lamps, plastic groundsheets, tarpaulins, candles and matches.

Accessibility considerations

When changing or allocating new storage areas to suit your needs better, consider the following:

- Store vacuum cleaners within easy reach.
- When building a new kitchen, make space for an equipment cupboard and appliance area.
- Keep a small tool kit within the home for small home repairs.
- When mounting clothes dryers or microwave ovens, ensure that they are within easy reach of everyone in the household.
- Ensure that all equipment is accessible to any disabled or elderly people in your household.
- Place items used regularly in cupboards in easily accessible places. Those used infrequently such as Christmas decorations and archive boxes can be stored in less accessible storage spots.

Some of my favourite storage ideas

See appendix B for the outlets mentioned below.

From Bayswiss

- round grass stool/storage box (large).

From Freedom Furniture

- Eton shoe bag (holds five pairs of shoes)
- chrome Monash 2 mobile robe — on wheels
- hand-woven 'Pandanus' tapered storage boxes
- hand-woven 'Pandanus' flip-top boxes
- 'Sanali' baskets in woven abaca
- 'Bucco' storage boxes with lids
- 'Sempurut' hand-woven rattan laundry baskets with removable canvas bag
- 'Kubico' CD storage units (four-, eight- or sixteen-drawer).

From kikki.K

- stationery boxes
- magazine boxes
- folders.

From Ikea

- Kabin shoe cabinet (holds 18 pairs)
- various other shoe cabinets and racks
- storage boxes in various sizes and colours.

From Orson & Blake

- leather storage boxes
- other storage boxes.

Part Three
Organising your office

19 Administration

> *With discipline comes organisation, strength of purpose, determination and success.*
> *Without discipline, there is disorganisation, confusion and failure...*
>
> Brian Adams

Your business is a reflection of you and what you stand for. Your office also reflects your business. If your office is messy, this will reflect on you. People have told me that if they walk into an untidy office, they immediately lose respect for the person who runs the business. The same goes for a cluttered desk or workspace. No matter how good you are at your job, your chances of promotion will be reduced if you can't organise your workspace or desk. Your boss and those around you may assume that if you are not able to organise yourself you won't be able to cope with more responsibilities.

Most people do not enjoy being disorganised. It can be

dissatisfying and embarrassing. Often, however, they don't know what to do about it or don't take the time to find out or try something new. It need not be difficult or expensive to create a stylish, organised and comfortable workspace. With the right knowledge and some common sense and creativity you can transform your office into a functional and efficient place.

Discipline

Practising discipline is a necessity in life. We have to be disciplined to get up in time to go to work each day or to take our children to school, to brush our teeth twice a day, to prepare and eat healthy meals, to exercise regularly and stay fit, and to learn something new. All this requires a certain amount of energy.

Discipline is defined in the *Macquarie Concise Dictionary* as:

> *Training to act in accordance with rules …The training effect of experience, adversity etc. A state of order maintained by training and control. A set or system of rules or regulations.*

Discipline is the action required to start being organised — to act physically with the intention to gain a result. Often we don't want to do a task such as organising our office space or kitchen cupboards because it's too hard or there's no time. We tend to say, 'I'd rather be out playing tennis with my friends.' With a little discipline, a plan of action and some positive energy, the task can be completed in no time. Anyone can be disciplined, especially as more often than not we have been trained as small children to work through tasks. This process is inside all of us — we just have to decide when we will take the action and do it!

Valuing the administration side of your business

Many companies allow their administration systems to let them down. This holds them back in reaching their full business potential. If there is no order or system, stress and frustration prevail and, most importantly, time and productivity are lost.

For example, all of a sudden your accountant telephones you, demanding tax information that she needs tomorrow. She has called many times and you've told her you'll get onto it. After repeated requests, a deadline is looming and now you have to put together information not only for your previous year's tax, but also for the year before that. You have no idea where to find all of the papers and receipts needed to give her the information. 'They're in a box somewhere,' you say. The truth is, if you had bothered to sort it out each month you wouldn't be in this mess.

Setting a process in place to ensure that this scenario never happens is quite simple. The administration side of your business can be likened to the engine room, and if it isn't in order, chances are the rest of your business will be suffering. Once you have key systems established, you will never have to worry again — provided you keep them running. If you don't have the time to handle a part of your business, outsource it or hire someone on a part-time basis.

Once every area of your business is in order, your productivity and efficiency will improve and you will have less stress to deal with. You will always know where you stand and be able to move forward more quickly towards your goals.

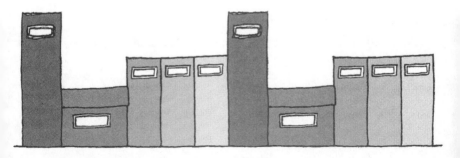

Organising a home office, systems and a backlog of actions items

'I'm so busy, and every time I go into my office I just can't think straight because of the clutter, which I don't have time to attend to. I travel for work and am away a lot. I haven't had time to invoice my clients and am owed thousands of dollars. I'd just love to be a bit more organised. Also, can you offer suggestions on how I can maximise my space in my office because it doubles as a guest bedroom.' — Robyn, in her forties, writer, busy social circle.

Robyn is generally a very organised woman, but hasn't been able to keep on top of organising her office and paperwork systems. She is too busy working, and doesn't have energy left over to put into the administration side of her business.

Robyn has a collection of storage boxes specifically to store paper clips, postage stamps, postcards and receipts. She has been keeping packaging boxes from designer stores and boutiques, so we use these to store items such as envelopes, rubber bands, pens, printed cards (with her name and address) and letterhead. Robyn also has very stylish archive boxes, which can be left on display in any room — perfect for storing articles she has written and memorabilia.

Robyn needs more filing areas (as she likes to use folders for her paperwork) so we discuss this and establish categories. I recommend diarising a timeframe to action items and pay bills, so she allocates a period of two hours per week to follow through with these processes.

The office space that Robyn works in is quite small and we are able to utilise unused wall space to maximise the storage space available. We designate a wall on which to group shelving, and this doubles the original shelf space.

Robyn is now able to send outstanding invoices to clients, amalgamate superannuation funds, and file paperwork. Everything now has a place. There is enough shelving available now for all her boxes and files and she now also has a process in place to invoice her clients immediately after she finishes a job.

All Robyn needed was routine in her life, a place for everything to live and better use of the space available. The last time I spoke to her she said she was managing better and was able to keep most things under control. Once the space had been cleared it was easier for her to walk into her office and just start work at her computer, without the stress of the clutter all around her. Even when things do get a little out of hand, all can be put back into place again in very little time.

20 Paperwork and filing systems

Have you ever been embarrassed when a client has phoned and you can't find their file? Do you often get frustrated by not being able to locate the right document when you need it? Do you cringe when customers come into your office because of the chaos and mess there? It's hard to respect a business professional you deal with or a colleague if their work environment looks chaotic and they constantly appear to operate in a disorganised way.

Their excuses and justifications are many. 'I know where everything is.' 'I like it like this.' 'I can find everything æ don't touch, because then I won't be able to find anything!' While some people have trouble keeping things in order and adjust themselves to their own disorganisation, the truth is that most would prefer to have a tidy, paper-free, organised office.

If you have problems keeping your office organised, it's time to do something about it! The steps in chapter 19 will help you to get started. In most cases you should only need to have on your desk a computer, a printer, a mouse-pad and one or two in-trays by the time you've finished. If you need regularly used information close at hand, you could have a work-in-progress file stand on your desk, for instance. Keep your immediate work space as free as possible from clutter from now on.

While it may seem difficult at first, with practice, throwing away will become easier.

Culling your filing system

Research has shown that 80 per cent of papers filed will never be looked at again. Ask yourself 'what would happen if I could not find this paper again?' Could you get the information somewhere else? If so, it won't be necessary to keep it. In many cases information held onto becomes outdated very quickly. Updated information can be obtained from the source, at your office, on the Internet or from your local library if it is absolutely necessary.

If your filing system is bulging at the seams and you haven't looked at most of the paperwork for over a year, work through it file by file or take everything out and store it in an archive box. In doing this you must plan to cull and sort all of it at a later date. Plan the date for a month or two away. Meanwhile, create your new system (see below). Then you will have a place to put items from the files that you decide to keep.

Steps to take when culling

1   *Start at the top drawer and work down.*
2   *Look at each hanging file to check its contents.*
         Keep documents that are important and discard those that are out of date or no longer relevant.
3   *Organise papers chronologically, with the most recent information at the front or top of the file.*
4   *Tidy as you go. Keep bank statements in folders provided by the appropriate bank. To secure information, use bull dog clips prefer ably (as they don't catch on other paperwork) or staples.*
5   *Each labelled hanging file should hold a labelled manilla folder to keep paperwork tidy so that it can be taken out easily. You will then know where in the system to return it.*
6   *Go through the whole drawer doing this. Archive or discard information that is outdated.*

When you have finished, marvel at the amount of space you have created already by throwing away outdated information and archiving 'must keep' information.

We have probably heard the advice about handling pieces of paper only once. An interesting exercise relayed to me via a friend who had attended a time management session was to put a red spot on each piece of paper on your desk or in your filing tray each time you touch or handle it. See how many times the same piece of paper gets handled before it's finally dealt with and filed, discarded or passed on to the next person in the chain. It's an interesting exercise to see how many pieces of paper develop the measles!

Creating a new filing system

Set up a filing system if you don't already have one. You will need a number of items.

- A filing cabinet with drawers: filing cabinets come in all shapes and sizes and usually have two, three or four drawers. You can buy simple cabinets made of aluminium, or beautiful cabinets made of steel, wood veneer or wood. You can have cabinets specially designed and built to suit your needs. Think about the material you prefer and ask an office furniture store to provide you with a quote for custom-building something different. This way you can have a unique office space that suits your character and needs.

- Hanging files: these can be bought in packets of twenty-five to fifty or boxes of fifty to one hundred at stationers and some newsagencies. They usually include crystal tabs (to house your label) and packets of labels, but check that these are included; if not, you will need to purchase them separately.

Manilla folders: these hold the information in your hanging file.

> *The only thing not to store in filing cabinets is bulky information such as large reports — unless you have the space available. Filing cabinets are designed to store paperwork in regular use.*

A newer style of filing system called a lateral filing system became available in Australia in the 1980s. The lateral filing system provides an alternative solution to filing. It is designed to save space and to increase efficiency when filing. It also looks modern, tidy and attractive. The system comprises a series of folders that sit next to each other on shelves with the end of the file facing the user, displaying the colour-coded labels that distinguish each folder.

Instead of pulling open a drawer, you can go straight to the required file on a shelf and pull it out. Doctors, lawyers and architects prefer this system of filing and retrieving information on a shelf rather than in a file drawer system. There are specialty companies providing this style of file system. You will find them in the *Yellow Pages* telephone directory under 'Office and Business Systems'.

Items for action

To store action items prior to processing, set up a folder with labelled dividers. When sorting the items you need to action, use the headings below:

- To Call
- To Pay
- To Read
- To Discuss
- To Write
- To Photocopy

Labelling new filing systems

I use a label machine to print out labels for my clients' filing systems. These can be purchased at stationery suppliers at a reasonable price. You can buy different coloured label tape to distinguish categories and sub-categories.

You can hand-write your labels, but make sure they can be read easily. It is easier to read 'title-case' letters (first letter in capitals, then lower case) rather than all 'upper-case' letters.

21 Archiving

Archive boxes can be found in all sizes and colours. Stationery suppliers will have a range of standard archive boxes that can be bought in bulk, but now there are many specialty stores and even supermarket chains selling storage boxes. I love to purchase appropriate sized wicker baskets with lids for my clients. They look attractive in the home office and blend with the decor.

In Australia, stores like Ikea, Big W and Target have 'designer' archive boxes, which are attractive and priced according to their style and material. If you don't have adequate storage space in your home and the archive boxes will be seen, it makes sense to have attractive boxes. Boxes can be made in leather, suede, stainless steel, rattan, wicker and fabrics of your choice.

Sorting and discarding information

Anything associated with your financial affairs and older than the *current* or *previous financial year* should be stored for five years. These are the current Australian Taxation Office regulations for record-keeping. Anything older than five years can be thrown away (or archived if you wish). Some people like to keep all their records, and that's OK too. It just means you have to record more information on your archive list.

Outdated information of a general nature can be thrown in the recycled paper box or bag, for example, old Frequent Flyer or airline newsletters, bank booklets and holiday brochures.

How to archive information

- Place the papers in a labelled manilla folder (unless they have their own specially made folder). Don't archive two-ring folders as they will take up too much space in archive boxes. Take the papers out and place them in manilla folders, labelling them appropriately.
- List the manilla folder names as you go and stack the folders into the archive box.
- Label the boxes Box 1, Box 2, etc. It is not necessary to list the contents on the outside of the box. Type up on your computer the list you have created and store it electronically. This makes updating easy. (If you don't

Corporate archiving

'We have five storerooms full of old records — some we have a list for and some we don't. We need to clear out these store-rooms and find out what we have and what we don't need any more so we can move to new premises and not pay for space that we don't necessarily need. We will also consider off-site storage for future archiving and want some recommendations about options.' — Thomas, a director of a film company with 50 staff.

Thomas, a company director, shows me around the company's offices and basement where their old information is stored. Ten years of paperwork has been stored in boxes and these are piled high, up to the door in most of the storage rooms, with limited access. A number of boxes have lists taped to the outside. Thomas informs me that a master list of contents is only available for approximately thirty boxes, relating to one department, and there are hundreds of boxes relating to four more departments that need to be recorded for future reference.

Thomas tells me that staff need to look back on records regularly. They realise they have been wasting time looking for information and want to avoid this in the future. A major part of this project is to ascertain whether any of the information is unnecessary now and can be culled.

A master list of the contents of each box is created and a new 'Archive System Register' document established on computer to record this.

Destruction dates are established for the information that is kept, so the company will have a future plan for destroying outdated papers. A confidential recycling company is contracted to take the outdated paper away.

At the end of the project, approximately five hundred boxes of information are taken from filing cabinets in the immediate office space, in addition to boxes stored in basement storerooms. The company assesses off-site storage options and decides to keep all their boxes off-site. They now have a master archive list to refer to in the office, and can recall files within an hour. Thomas feels more in control and clearer about moving premises now. The staff are happier. Procedures are written to show them how to manage future archiving. They have less clutter in their filing cabinets and more space around them, and they are more able to concentrate on their jobs.

have a computer, write a neat list and keep it in the front hanging file of your filing cabinet with your file drawer list.)

When you need to retrieve anything, open your document and search for a key word. In Microsoft Word, click on the Edit icon then the 'find' function and enter the key word, for example, 'tax information'. You can use the control key and 'f' for this function. Once you have found the key word you will be able to see which box the item is in. (To ensure that you don't lose documents from your computer, do a back-up on a disk or CD-ROM. Label your back-up copy and keep it in a disk box in your office.)

22 Home offices

Depending on the nature of your work you don't necessarily need a lot of space to run a small business. If you are adequately equipped and have what you need at your fingertips, you should be able to run most businesses efficiently from an area of your home.

When planning to work from home, try to set up your home office in a quiet room or area of the house. If you need to adapt part of a room for your business and this room serves a dual purpose, have a good storage area to store office items out of sight once you have finished your work. If you are running a business where you need to have clients visit you, ensure that your office looks as professional as possible and try to keep the office area separate from the rest of the house.

For instance, if your spare bedroom is near your front door, it would make sense to utilise this space for your office. In this way you won't have clients wandering through your personal living space to your office at the back of the house. Another alternative if you are using a back room as a home office is to have rear access. Indicate this on your gate or at your front door.

Hang beautiful fabrics around the edge of tables or purpose-built desks to hide storage boxes and decorate your office in the process. Make your office visually appealing. The more you like your surroundings the more you will feel happy to be working there.

You will have to purchase equipment to be able to run your home office efficiently. The following list serves as a guide.

Equipment required when setting up a home office

- *answering machine (I prefer to use a Messagebank service so I don't need this equipment)*
- *bookshelves (for storing reference books, arch files, phone books)*
- *calculator*
- *clock*

- *comfortable chair(s) (ergonomically designed if you spend a lot of time at your desk or computer)*
- *computer*
- *contact record file or address book*
- *desk(s)*
- *desk lamp (adjustable)*

- diary
- fax machine (some also also function as phones and photocopiers)
- filing cabinet or shelving for lateral files
- noticeboard
- paper trays
- photocopier (optional depending on the needs of your business)
- portable voice recorder
- printer
- rubbish bin
- scanner (can double as a photocopier for small businesses)
- shelving (preferably with lockable doors to keep articles dust-free and secure)
- stationery
- telephone(s)
- trolley (sometimes needed in a busy office to avoid back strain)
- workbench (for preparing layouts of proposals or work in progress)

Stationery supplies

This is a list of the stationery items that are needed to run most businesses. Keep these items on hand so you will always have anything you need when you need it.

- archive boxes
- book for recording telephone messages and conversations (loose paper gets misplaced)
- business card folder or box
- business card holder
- CD storage box
- dictionary
- drawer organiser
- envelopes (different sizes for different uses; buy standard-size envelopes in bulk boxes)
- eraser (rubber)
- Express Post envelopes

- floppy disk box
- foldback clips (better known as bulldog clips)
- folders (two-ring or display folders in various sizes)
- glue
- hanging files and label inserts
- highlighter pens (various colours)
- hole punch (you may require a few of varying sizes)
- ink cartridges (for printer and fax machines)
- letter opener
- Liquid Paper or other brand correction fluid or tape
- magazine files (for storing business magazines, bulky reports, catalogues)
- manilla folders
- marker pens (black, blue and red)
- mouse pad
- packing tape
- pads of paper (for writing notes, meeting information and client information)
- pins (drawing pins, coloured map pins)
- paper clips
- paper for printer, fax machine and photocopier
- pencil sharpener
- pencils
- pens
- plastic sheet protectors (useful for protecting loose paper and letters)
- postage stamps
- Post-it notes (various sizes)
- ruler
- scissors
- Stanley knife (for all sorts of uses)
- stapler
- staples
- staple remover
- sticky tape
- wall planner

Tips for home offices

Design a stationery order form and keep it with your stationery
catalogues or stationery file, or simply store it on your computer.
Every time you need to order an item, enter it on your form then
put the form in your stationary file until you place your next
order. This way you won't have to go through the time-consuming
process of checking your stock on the day you plan to order. You
can design a simple form in Microsoft software (Word or Excel), or,
depending on the size and nature of your business, you may
choose to install specific software on your computer to take care of
and monitor supplies. Check the packages available with your
computer dealer.

Tips for small businesses with staff

Assign to one staff member the task of ordering all your office
equipment and stationery supplies. Provide one key to the
stationery cabinet to this staff member so that all staff have to
obtain stationery from them. The person in this position will have
the task of recording and monitoring all stock taken from the
stationery cabinet amd reordering regularly.

Tips for a one-person small business

You may wish to use a mail service company such as Mail Boxes. These services provide mail collection (you pay so much per year for a mail box on their premises); a pick-up and drop-off point for courier services; and access to commercial photocopying machines (usually via a smart card for self-service operation at a much cheaper rate than a pharmacy or newsagent, and with faster machines). These services usually have colour photocopying facilities on site and offer services such as 'stuffing' envelopes for mail-outs.

Tips for everyone

Set up a recycling area in your office so everyone has a place to put used paper and plastic. Most corporate offices will have a recycling procedure, but in a small home office environment you can use empty boxes to store excess paper and waste before recycling it. Ensure that your staff know where to put waste materials to protect the integrity of your business.

23 Lists

> *Go confidently in the direction of your dreams — live the life you've imagined!*
>
> Thoreau

Keeping a list is an important way of remembering what you need to buy when food-shopping or gift-buying, or things you need to achieve each week. It is a simple concept that is easy to do. All you need is some paper and a pen.

I couldn't survive without my 'things to do' list. I consider it a waste of brain space if I have to remember too many details, so I write on a list any information that I want to recall later. The same applies when I am organising a client. One of my key tasks at the outset is to write a list for the client of what needs doing, so they can make progress during an organising session.

As well as daily, weekly, monthly and yearly lists there are also special lists æ checklists that are only updated if things change such as your wallet contents list or important documents list. You can have lists for a variety of purposes and these may cover a variety of timeframes. For example:

- ☼ Daily lists: List food to purchase, people to telephone or e-mail.

- ☼ Weekly lists: List birthday presents to buy or cards to send, children's activities to prepare, appointments to be attended, school excursions to prepare for and special television programs to watch.

- ☼ Monthly lists: List bill payments to make, group activities or projects to participate in, gardening to do, entertainment to plan, sport to play and people to see.

- ☼ Yearly lists: List school holiday periods to plan for, birthday and anniversary dates to remember, holidays to plan and events, entertainment and development activities to attend.

Once you have a list, you can prioritise the tasks on it as follows:

- ☼ A: Must do
- ☼ B: Should do
- ☼ C: Would be nice to do

Create a list of all the documents that are important in your life. It is a good idea to photocopy them, keeping a copy for yourself in your 'important documents' file at home or at your office. Place the original document in a safe deposit box at your bank. Alternatively, purchase a small home safe and have it installed in a secure and discreet place. If there is an emergency or disaster, such as a bushfire or flood where there is a possibility that everything might be destroyed, it will be a relief to be able to locate these documents easily. It will also be helpful for family members to know where everything of importance is kept. Send an additional copy of your important documents to your solicitor, a friend or a family member living in another area.

Include copies of:

- birth, death and marriage certificates
- divorce papers
- car registration papers
- citizenship papers
- contracts
- family history charts
- insurance policies: home and contents, life, car
- investments: share and bond certificates, deeds and mortgage papers
- leases
- passports
- superannuation fund policies
- wills.

You may wish to include the negatives of photos that are important to you.

Lists that can be used regularly

Prepare these lists on your computer and print them out when you need them.

- birthday and anniversary dates
- camping essentials
- child-minding/carer information (information about how to care for your child)
- children's school holiday periods
- Christmas cards (who you sent cards to last year and who sent them to you)
- e-mailing list (to keep track of e-mails sent and e-mails awaiting responses)
- food shopping
- gardening (seasonal planting)
- house-minding information (how you want everything to be looked after)
- house renovation tasks
- inventory of contents of wallet
- subscription or membership expiry dates
- theatre subscription booking dates

Home disaster plan

With the world's weather patterns changing, you can never be sure when you may be faced with a disaster that has the potential to destroy your home and its contents. Therefore, it is worthwhile to have an emergency plan should you ever need to evacuate your home in the event of a fire, storm or flood.

First, make sure you know where each of the following important documents or personal belongings is located in your home. If you are given advance warning for evacuation, take full advantage of this time to gather all important belongings and place them in your car.

Essential items to take

This list of important documents or personal belongings includes the items that I consider imperative to take from your home when being evacuated. Consider the time it would take to replace all of these records and possessions if you had to.

- current tax year tax papers
- cheque books and statements
- house property title
- home insurance policy
- home contents insurance policy
- superannuation folder
- current shares folder
- investment papers
- photograph albums and photo boxes

- important papers such as marriage certificate, birth certificates, passports
- collections such as stamps, coins etc.
- computer hard-drive
- pocket PC
- mobile phones
- laptop computer
- wallet
- spare sets of clothes (for all weather conditions)
- toiletries
- cameras
- valuable artwork
- tapes and CDs
- past tax papers
- back-up disks and CD-ROMs
- software CD-ROMs
- watch
- current work assignment papers
- briefcase

Important contacts

Each of us needs a personal phone directory. The following is a sample of a list that can be used to store all your important contact information. This will provide you and your family with a ready reference when you need it. Alternatively, design your own to suit your needs perfectly.

Fill in the relevant information as soon as possible to save yourself time when you need a telephone number.

Keep this directory list taped to the inside of your pantry door or in the front page of a display folder that everyone in the house knows about (including your youngest child). In the event of an emergency they will know where to look for the appropriate telephone number.

List of tradespeople and important telephone contacts

Tradesperson relative/friend /service	Contact name	Allocated time for services	Telephone numbers
Accountant			Office:
			Mobile:
After-school care			Office:
			Mobile:
Ambulance			Emergency: Dial 000
			Local hospital:
Aunty			Home:
			Mobile:
Babysitter			Home:
			Mobile:
Banker			Office:
			Mobile:
Chemist			Shop:
Cleaner			Office:
			Mobile:
Day-care kindergarten			Office:
			Mobile:
Dentist			Office:
			Mobile:
Directory assistance			Office:
Doctor			Office:
			Mobile:

Electrician	Office:
	Mobile:
Fire brigade	Emergency: Dial 000
	Office:
Gardener	Office:
	Mobile:
Grandparents	Home:
	Mobile:
Grandparents	Home:
	Mobile:
Gymnasium	Office:
	Mobile:
Hairdresser	Salon:
	Mobile:
Hospital (nearest)	Emergency: Dial 000
	Office:
Lawn-mowing service	Office:
	Mobile:
Maintenance service	Office:
	Mobile:
Nanny	Office:
	Mobile:
Neighbour (left) #1	Home:
	Mobile:
Neighbour (right) #2	Home:
	Mobile:
Police	Emergency: Dial 000
	Local station:
Plumber	Office:
	Mobile:

For example:

| *Professional* | *Get Organised* | *Wednesdays -* | *Office:* (02) 9949-3065 |
| *organiser* | *Carol Posener* | *9.30-1.30 (4 hrs)* | *Mobile:* 0414 975 657 |

School/s   Office:
                                                Mobile:
Solicitor   Office:
                                                Mobile:
Stockbroker   Office:
                                                Mobile:
Taxi service   Depot:
Uncle   Home:
                                                Mobile:
Veterinary clinic   Office:
                                                AH emergency:
Window cleaner   Office:
                                                Mobile:
Work — Dad   Office:
                                                Mobile:
Work — Mum   Office:
                                                Mobile:
Yoga teacher   Office:
                                                Mobile:

Fire evacuation: steps to take

The following four steps provide general evacuation guidelines. For further advice, contact your local fire authority. As a general precautionary principle, it is essential to keep gutters clean and free from leaves if you live close to bush. Do this regularly or have it done by your lawn-mowing contractor.

Stage 1: Preparing for evacuation

- Put on long pants (in wool, cotton or denim) and a long-sleeved top (preferably in wool or cotton). Wear strong shoes and socks to protect against hot embers and broken glass. Avoid shorts and short-sleeved tops — you need to protect your skin. Avoid synthetic clothing: if it burns it will stick to the skin and increase the depth of the burn.
- Put on a hat (in wool or cotton).
- Locate gloves and goggles.
- Fit all hoses to taps. (Ensure that you have hose nozzles.)
- Fill the bath and spa early (as tap water may stop altogether before the fire gets to you).
- Place wet towels around the garden and the house.
- Close all windows.
- Put ladders up to the roof.
- Wet down timber areas.

- Clean out the gutters.
- Block the gutters with rags and fill them with water.
- Wet tea-towels for use as face masks. (Draping wet towels or blankets around you can protect you against heat and burning.)
- Put on gloves and goggles if there is a lot of smoke.

Remember, it is highly likely that there will be NO water (not just low water pressure, but NO water at all) as fire-fighters will have access to the water supply for fire-fighting.

Stage 2: Packing up cars

- Using the list on page 195, gather possessions and important documents.
- Put the items carefully in your car so they can't be damaged when you drive off.
- Cover the contents with a blanket.

Stage 3: Getting out

- Turn the phone message answering machine on.
- Notify police that you have evacuated the house.
- Lock up the house.
- Go to the agreed or specified assembly point.
- Call your closest relative.

Stage 4: Coming back

- Check for any fire damage.
- Check for any looting.
- Check the path of the fire to ascertain the likelihood of the fire turning back on your home.
- Unpack the cars when it is safe to do so.

Be aware that outbreaks may occur later. Check all areas of your home to ensure that there are no embers still burning that could reignite.

Emergencies: power loss and blackouts

Have the following close at hand in a cupboard:

- spare water
- batteries for torches
- torches that work
- candles (different sizes with appropriate holders)
- matches
- hurricane lanterns with supplies of oil or kerosene (kept in your garage or shed — make sure they are stored safely).

24 Making the most of technology

> *Live the life you dream!*
>
> Anon

Technological changes have given us some compact solutions to organising our lives. Thirty-five years ago computers were the size of a small dining room; now they can fit neatly into a tiny microchip and take up only a small section of your credit card.

Electronic personal organisers

Portable electronic personal organisers the size of the palm of your hand are designed to manage the information in your life and save you carrying around a diary, address book and notepad. You type in information with a pen-like instrument and can take notes, hold contact details, manage your calendar, make lists, store anniversary reminders or create your own reminders and e-mails. Some have Internet connection. You can also view and edit spreadsheets, documents, videos and photos, and browse Web contents offline. Brands to look for include Palm (PalmPilot), Apple Newton, Sharp Wizard and IBM.

Software to consider

You can set up an efficient way to record data about all your clients with specially designed software called contact relationship databases. Some of the records you will be able to recall are your client information, the last date and time you contacted the client and the conversation you had. You can then set a reminder in place to appear on your screen on the day you need to call them. Each time you e-mail the client, a copy of the e-mail is stored with the contact information for future reference. This saves you having to search for a specific e-mail elsewhere.

Software can be designed to do just about any task you want, but you can purchase ready-made software designed specifically for certain tasks. Take advantage of these products. Once you know how to use them they will speed up processes for you and keep your life in order and flowing efficiently.

There are many products in the marketplace so contact your computer dealer and ask them to recommend one that meets your needs.

Getting organised on the Internet

The Internet hit Australia in the early 1990s and has since become a necessity for many people. Now it is the biggest information resource available to everyone, superseding libraries. It allows us to access information and services worldwide without having to leave the comfort of our own homes. It can be a valuable time-saving tool provided you understand how to use it effectively and what information is available to you. Any of the following tasks can be done on the Internet, saving you precious time:

- banking
- buying books, gifts, greeting cards, music, newspapers and magazines and theatre tickets
- checking movie times, sports results and the weather
- downloading application forms (rather than ordering them on the telephone and then waiting for them to arrive by mail)
- learning languages
- listening to the radio
- looking up telephone numbers in the *Yellow Pages* and *White Pages*. (This function saves you time because it enables you to access all the information about that telephone number, including name and address details, and even print out a street map of the location.)

- moving house — organising a removalist and accessing tips on packing and storing possessions
- on-line auctioning
- paying wages and bills
- purchasing airline tickets and booking travel and accommodation
- redeeming Frequent Flyer points
- searching for information about products
- searching for property (both rentals and sales)
- shopping for food and groceries.

Many people are reluctant to use the Internet as they see it as something new and confronting. It is worthwhile to enrol in a training session to be shown the general functions it will do and how to access information easily. The Internet will open up a whole new world to you. Once you start using it, you will discover how easy it is: just 'follow your nose', as the instructions are generally clear.

Internet service providers (ISPs) include Big Pond, Ozemail, TPG and Primus, to name a few. Start getting organised on the Internet — it will save you loads of time.

 Mark your favourite and most used Websites for future ease of access. If you find a Website that you know you will refer to again, click on 'Favorites' from the toolbar at the top of the page and then click on 'Add to Favorites'.

Computer viruses

Computer viruses are being created worldwide every day and sent via the Internet to cause havoc with computer systems that are vulnerable. They will infect your computer and can destroy all the information on it. Viruses are generally sent through attachments to e-mails. Never open attachments unless you are certain of their origin. Delete them and empty them from the deleted items folder.

It is essential that you purchase a virus scan software package if you are using the Internet, including e-mailing. You will need to download updates to your anti-virus software from the Internet each day before you do any work on your computer. Also download full new versions as soon as they are available. In this way you can be sure you have done all you can to protect yourself from any new viruses that might have been created and sent out overnight from anywhere in the world.

Anti-virus software will sift through your files daily to check that everything is performing as it should and cull out any 'bugs' or viruses. Similar to an insurance policy, such software will give you peace of mind as long as you are diligent about downloading the updates and running the software daily. It is also worth consulting an IT specialist to check that the software is compatible with your computer protocols.

25 Innovative ideas for the future

Designers are coming up with some great concepts for space-saving and time-saving devices. Here are some ideas to think about.

I used to love to watch 'The Jetsons' cartoon on television when I was a child. The cartoon was about the life of a space-age family and their space-age home with all its efficient time-saving devices, including moving walkways — all 'out of this world' to us back then.

Miraculously, much of this fantasy world has now become a reality. It only goes to prove the adage 'whatever the mind can conceive, it can achieve'. An Australian company, SmartWorld, has designed two very innovative products called 'ThinkBoxx' and 'HomeBoxx'

ThinkBoxx

The ThinkBoxx is the world's most intelligent home automation controller. It allows you to activate your home security, lighting, heating, cooling, entertainment, garden irrigation, curtains and blinds from any touchpad in the home or by remote control from any touch tone or mobile phone inside or away from the home. It can also be voice-activated.

Imagine you are at work and decide to invite some colleagues home for dinner that night. You pick up your telephone or go to your office computer keyboard and press the numbers '2, 5, 7, 9', the numbers you have selected activate your 'ThinkBoxx'. Your home lights, irrigation, music and temperature controls are all set in motion ready for when you arrive. As you approach your home, your gates slowly open. Cruising into your fairy-lit driveway, you admire your beautiful garden, freshly watered by the irrigation system. As you enter the house with your friends, your choice of music filters from every room and the temperature of the house is a perfect 21°. How much more comfortable and organised can you get!

HomeBoxx

The HomeBoxx, which is a small box built into a wall of your home, is an all-inclusive lifestyle management centre or hub. All services from the outside world, including gas, power, telephone lines and security alarm facilities, enter through it and are distributed throughout the home. The HomeBoxx acts as the control centre for all your appliances. (See appendix B for the SmartWorld Corporation Limited Website for more information about the ThinkBoxx and HomeBoxx technology.)

The Besk

The Besk is a desk that converts into a double bed. It was featured at the 100% Design Exhibition in London at the end of 2001. Its space-saving design makes it ideal for use in small apartments, studios or bed-sit apartments, or in an average home as a spare double bed for overnight visitors.

The Besk represents the optimum in furniture design and manufacture. It can be put together by one person in less than fifteen minutes from four factory-assembled elements.

Besk tops and futons come in a number of finishes to suit the decor of any home. Made from long-lasting quality materials, including aluminium and solid wood, the Besk features a luxury mattress that is the thickness of a normal bed mattress but designed to be light.

The Besk stocks a range of Besk pedestals designed to fit under the desk — great for extra storage. (See appendix B for contact details.)

World-class survival tools

The need for tools can present itself at any time. Imagine how organised you will be if you carry a small set of tools in your wallet.

Most people have heard about the Swiss Army Knife and its versatility and uses. The designers of this knife, Victorinox in Switzerland, are now producing a range called Victorinox® SwissCard®. This revolutionary product is truly multifunctional. About the same size as a credit card, it can sit in your wallet along with your other cards. It features a small blade, scissors, a ballpoint pen, a nail file/screwdriver tip, a mini-ruler, a stainless steel pin, a toothpick and tweezers. It is brilliant, easy to use and space-saving. (See appendix B for their Website details and range of SwissCards®.)

There are clever people in our world coming up with brilliant ideas to save us time and help us get organised into the twenty-first century. Next we'll be dialling numbers into our touch phones to program our personal computerised home robots to prepare and cook our meals or fill our baths for our arrival home. As you are driving home from work you'll smile and think to yourself, 'Now all I have to do tonight is relax — thank you, technology. I've got the life!'

Conclusion

Organising is an ongoing life process, so there is no quick-fix solution. To organise yourself you will need to make a choice to change your life, have a positive attitude, prepare yourself mentally for the change and be determined to see results. Organising yourself is also about simplifying the possessions in your life and keeping them under control — not letting them control you.

If you've organised your life to a point where everything is in order, you will feel you have achieved a balance and you will love your life. Limitless possibilities will open up and you will be able to lead your life free of the restrictions that disorder brings. Being organised will also help you to cope with any difficulties that may arise in your life.

A few things may happen as result of getting your life in order:

- Your relationships may become more secure because you have taken the time to address your personal issues.
- You may identify the need, and include time each day, to develop yourself spiritually to enhance your busy life, relieving stress and giving you holistic balance.
- You will have more time to spend with your family and other important people.
- You will have more time to pursue life-long passions such

as learning something new, writing a book or travelling.

- You will have time to exercise so you will be fitter and healthier.
- You will have more time for socialising and for doing fun things such as holding parties.

Being organised is about making the time to do things that are important to you. It is about having greater freedom and choice. It liberates you from chaos and allows you to work towards attaining the lifestyle that you dream of, and that you know you deserve. So take the first step and get your life organised.

Appendix A   Avenues for disposal

Recycling

National

Amcor Recycling Australasia recycles paper and cardboard. Phone: 1800 819 000; Website: www.amcor.com.au

Corporate Recycling is all about recycling office consumable waste such as fax, copier and printer cartridges or bottles, also paper, cardboard, glass, aluminium cans, plastic, computers and printers, scrap metal, oil and fluorescent tubes. They have offices in NSW, Victoria, South Australia, Tasmania and Western Australia. Website: www.corporaterecycling.com.au

The *Mobile Phone Industry Recycling Program* runs during National Recycling Week, annually in November. For more information see www.amta.org.au/recycle

SCRAP (School Communities Recycling All Paper) was established to encourage schools, children and the wider community to become more environmentally friendly. They run many different recycling programs (not just paper). Website: www.nccnsw.org.au/member.scrap/ or www.nccnse.org.au

The *Salvation Army* accepts clothing, homeware, furniture and some electrical goods. Phone: 131 640

NSW

All Paper Destruction will destroy office files, computer paper and large quantities of other paper. Phone: 02 9725 3959

Australian Plastics Re-Processing Pty Ltd recycles plastics. Phone: 02 9833 8655

The *Bower Reuse and Repair Centre* is a charity and community-based group formed to offer an alternative to throwing items out for council collection (where everything then goes to the tip). They collect for free, then repair and recycle furniture (indoor/outdoor), whitegoods, building materials, kitchenware and electrical appliances. They also hold workshops to show you how to repair and update items. Phone: 02 9568 6280; Website: http://home.pacific.net.au/~thebower

MRI Australia Pty Ltd recycles electrical equipment, such as televisions, computers, telecommunications (including mobile phones) and batteries. Phone: 02 9729 4999

Reverse Garbage Co-operative is a non-profit organisation that collects industrial refuse that would normally be used for landfill. They also collect imperfectly made products and refuse from factories to on-sell to the creative community. Phone 02 9569 3132 or 02 9600 9291.

Revolve Centre was set up by Lismore Council and Hendersons Scrap Metal to reduce landfill at the tip. They recycle anything that has come from the tip face, such as computers, furniture, antiques, industrial waste, stereos, video recorders and televisions. Phone: 02 6622 0895

The *Smith Family* accepts clothing, homewares, linen, blankets and CDs. Phone: 02 9550 4422 or the number for your state or region.

St Vincent de Paul accepts clothing, homewares and furniture. Phone: 02 9560 8666 or the number for your state or region; Website: www.vinnies.org.au

The *Total Environment Centre* is an environmental advocacy group. It can offer tips on avenues for disposal. Phone: 02 9299 5599; Website: www.tec.nccnsw.org.au

VIC

The *Brotherhood of St Lawrence* will accept secondhand clothing, furniture, electrical goods and linen in good condition. Phone: 03 9385 6111 (furniture), 03 9464 4633 (clothing and household goods)

Reverse Art Truck is a non-profit association in Ringwood that collects and distributes industrial off-cuts and art & craft materials to on-sell back to the community. Phone: 03 9879 1264 or 03 5995 3168

QLD

Reverse Garbage Co-operative operates the same as the Reverse Garbage Co-operative in Sydney, above. Phone: 07 3844 9744

ACT

Revolve is a non-profit organisation that collects reusable items from the tip face to resell to the public. Members of the public can drop off items directly, and there is also a pick up service. Phone: 02 6239 3691

TAS

Resource Work Co-operative Society is a non-profit organisation that will collect anything reusable off the tip face such as timber, clothing, furniture, electrical goods, computers and old telecommunication items, and then resell them. People can also drop off reusable items to be sold at the Tip Shop. Better quality items are sold at the Collectables shop in Hobart. Phone: 03 6234 3772 or 03 6224 8669 (for the Tip Shop) or 03 6231 4838 (for Collectables)

WA

Waste Wise WA will give you all the information you need on recycling and reducing waste. Phone: 08 9222 8666; Website: www.wastewise.wa.gov.au

Government authorities
Federal Government

Environment Australia. Phone: 1800 065 823; Website: www.ea.gov.au

State and Territory Governments

NSW (For suppliers of recycled products for sale.) Phone: 131 555; Website: www.livingthing.net.au

VIC (Environment Protection Authority) Phone: 03 9695 2700 or Website: www.epa.vic.gov.au

QLD Phone: 07 3227 7111; Website: www.env.qld.gov.au

ACT Phone: 02 6207 9000; Website: www.environment.act.gov.au

TAS Phone: 03 6233 8011; Website: www.dpiwe.tas.gov.au

WA Phone: 08 9222 7000; Website: www.environ.wa.gov.au

SA Phone: 08 8204 2004; Website: www.environment.sa.gov.au/epa

NT Phone: 08 8924 4139; Website: www.lpe.nt.gov.au

Appendix B Resources and suppliers

Storage Shops and Products — Australia

Abbey Design Living has sturdy handcrafted boxes to stow trinkets, keepsakes and photos. Phone: 08 8373 2013.

Bayswiss has containers and other ideas for storage. Phone: 02 9368 0222 (Moore Park, NSW) or 02 9326 0111 (hotline); Website: www.bayswiss.com.au

Book Sling is a book storage idea. Designer: Anna Burnett, London, UK. Supplier in Sydney: Katie Burnett. Phone: 02 9973 3454; Website: www.ushuus.co.uk

Compact Business Systems is an information management and business processes company specialising in electronic and lateral filing systems. Phone: 02 9310 1700; Website: www.compactsystems.com.au

Freedom Furniture supplies storage products. Phone 1300 135 588; Website: www.freedom.com.au

Howard's Storage World supplies storage products. Phone: 1300 666 616; Website: www.howardsstorageworld.com.au

Ikea specialises in storage and space-saving ideas. Phone: 02 9418 2744.

Kikki.K stocks a range of office stationery and storage boxes. Phone: 03 9676 2998; Website: www.kikki-k.com.au

KIFKAF has a unique selection of Vietnamese storage containers. Phone: 02 9699 3499; Website: www.kifkaf.com.au

MH *Way & Co.* specialises in space-saving briefcases, diaries, notebooks, document holders, tubes for carrying drawings; bags for travel, computers and presentations. Phone: 02 9233 1065; Website: www.mhway.it; e-mail: Sydney Showroom, mhwayandco@bigpond.com

Orson & Blake has storage baskets and ideas. Phone: 02 8399 2525 (Surry Hills, NSW), 02 9326 1155 (Woollahra, NSW).

Papaya has storage ideas and home office storage. Phone: 02 9362 1620.

Pentimento has storage boxes. Phone: 02 9565 5591 (Newtown, NSW).

Spacemaster Office Systems supplies lateral filing systems, shelving and storage solutions, workstations and chairs. Phone Toll Free: 1800 555 633; Website: www.spacemaster.com.au

Victorinox® SwissCard® (card-size tool kit) is distributed by Sheldon & Hammond Pty Ltd. Website: www.victorinox.com

Trusty Cases & Boxes supplies storage boxes for all situations and customised packaging. Phone: 02 9907 1511; Website: www.trusty.com.au

Storage shops and products — international

Smythson of Bond Street stocks leather diaries, boxes, portable leather writing desks and travel cabinets. Phone: 44 (0) 8705

211 311 (London); Website: www.smythson.com

The Besk is a desk that converts into a double bed. Designer: Antony Dixon, UK. Phone: 44 (0) 870 752 4842; e-mail: info@besk.co.uk; Website: www.besk.co.uk

The Conran Shop has storage ideas and products. London, New York, Paris, Tokyo. Website: www.conran.com

Electronic solutions

ACT Software supplies contacts/relationship database software. Phone: Eyecatcher Solutions, 02 9439 8264; Website: www.act.com

Compact Business Systems is an information management and business processes company specialising in electronic document management, lateral filing systems, disaster recovery solutions, and imaging and scanning hardware. Phone: 02 9310 1700; Website: www.compactsystems.com.au

LG Electronics supplies digital home networks and home automation systems. Phone Toll Free: 1800 643 156: Website: www.lge.com.au

SmartWorld Corporation Ltd supplies home automation systems (ThinkBoxx and HomeBoxx technology). Phone: 08 8340 9971; Website: www.smart.com.au

Home-delivered food and beverage shopping via the Internet

Coles supermarkets sell food and alcohol via the Internet.

Website: www.colesonline.com.au

Greengrocer.com offers gourmet fruit and vegetable shopping. Website: www.greengrocer.com

Shopfast supplies food, CDs and books via the Internet. Website: www.shopfast.com

Simon Johnson sells quality food in-store, or order by phone or on the Internet. Phone: 1800 655 622 or 02 9328 6888 (Woollahra, NSW); Website: www.simonjohnson.com.au

Woolworths supermarkets sells food and alcohol via the Internet. Website: www.homeshop.com.au

Further reading

Chic Simple — Desk, Kim Johnson Gross & Jeff Stone, Thames & Hudson, Great Britain, 1994.

Chic Simple — Storage, Kim Johnson Gross & Jeff Stone, Thames & Hudson, Great Britain, 1994.

Clear Your Clutter with Feng Shui, Karen Kingston, Judy Piatkus (Publishers), London, 1998.

Clearing the Clutter — 100 Ways to Energize your Life, Mary Lambert, Cima Books, London, 2001.

Courage to be Rich, The, Suze Orman, Bantam Books, Sydney, 2000.

Making the Most of Workspaces, Lorrie Mack, Conran Octopus, London, 1995.

100 House-Keeping Hints, Jean McGlone & Daphne Metland, Octopus Books, London, 1984.

Organise Yourself, Ronni Eisenberg with Kate Kelly, Judy Piatkus (Publishers), London, 1990.

Organized Living, Dawna Walter with Helen Chislett, Conran Octopus, London, 1997.

Organizing from the Inside Out, Julie Morgenstern, Hodder Headline, Sydney, 2000.

Organizing Your Workspace, Odette Pollar, Crisp Publications, California, 1992.

Storage — Stylish Solutions for Every Room in Your Home, Joanna Copestick & Meryl Lloyd, Murdoch, London, 1998.

Storage (Home Design Workbooks), Dinah Hall & Barbara Weiss, Dorling Kindersley, London, 1997.

Storage Made Easy, Candace Ord Manroe, Reader's Digest, New York, 1995.

The Home Office Book, Donna Paul, Artisan, New York, 1996.

The Ultimate Book of Organizing Hints & Tips, Cassandra Kent, Dorling Kindersley, London, 1997.

Index